OLD CAVES

Art Direction: Tom Kaczynski
Production: Az Sperry

UNCIVILIZED BOOKS
P. O. Box 6534
Minneapolis, MN 55406
USA
uncivilizedbooks.com

First Edition, June 2023

10 9 8 7 6 5 4 3 2 1

ISBN 978-1-941250-53-2

DISTRIBUTED TO THE TRADE BY:
Consortium Book Sales & Distribution, LLC.
34 Thirteenth Avenue NE, Suite 101
Minneapolis, MN 55413-1007
cbsd.com
Orders: (800) 283-3572

Printed in China

innoVationpei

OLD CAVES

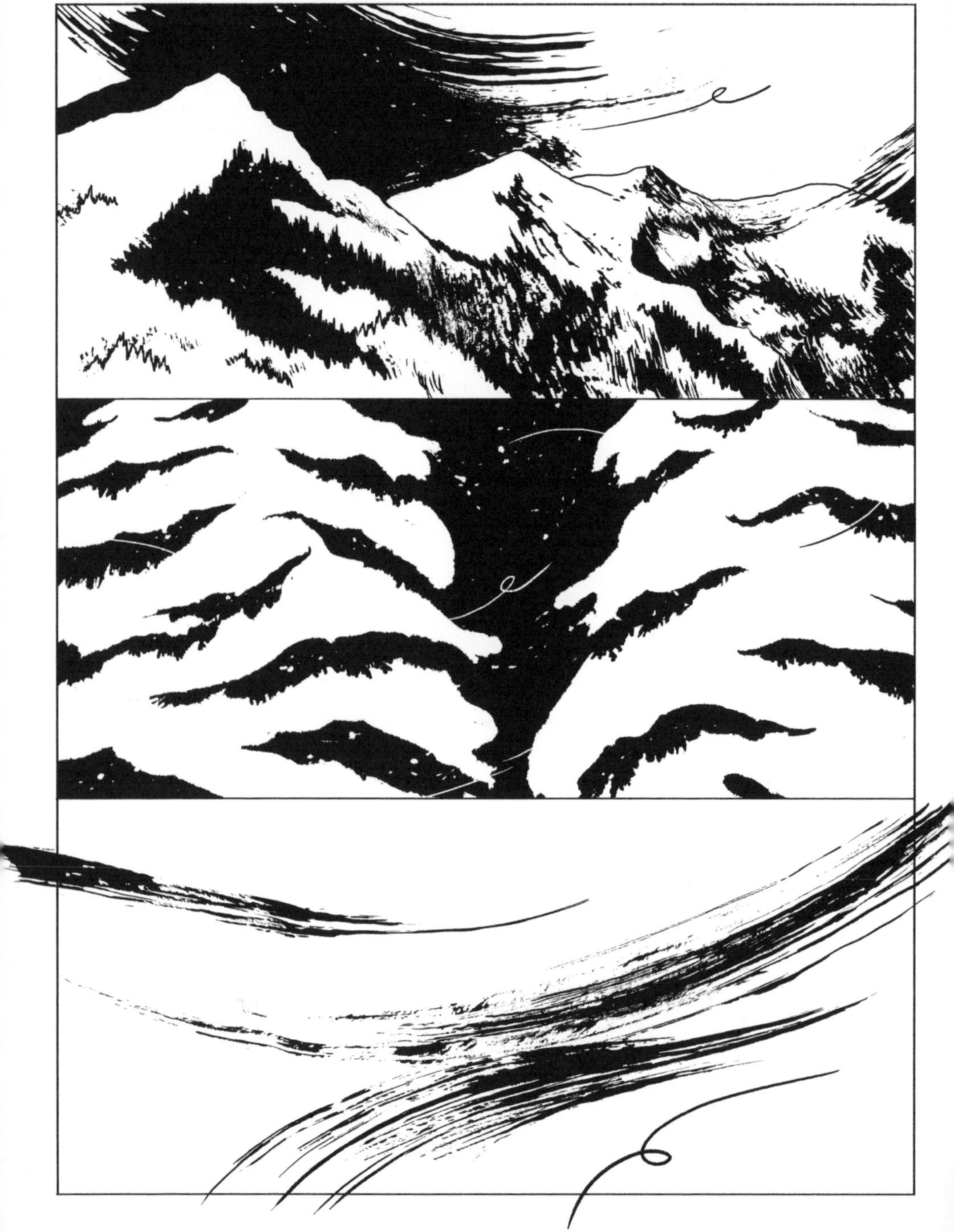

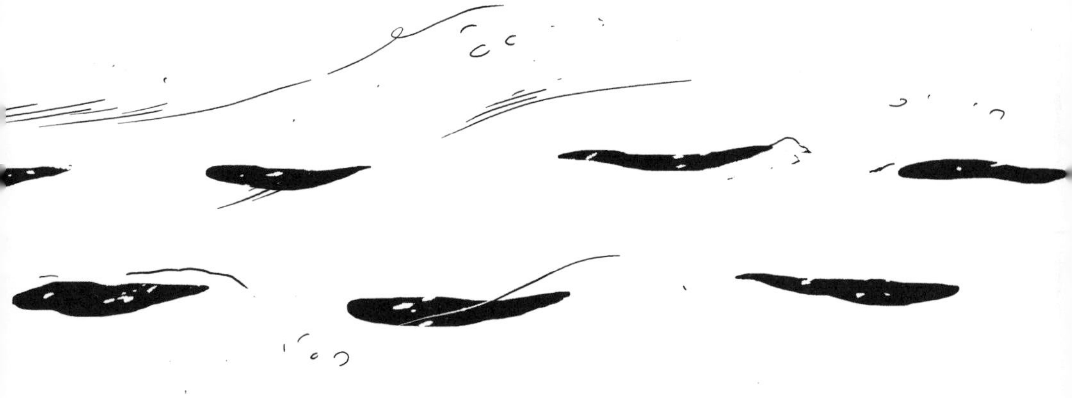

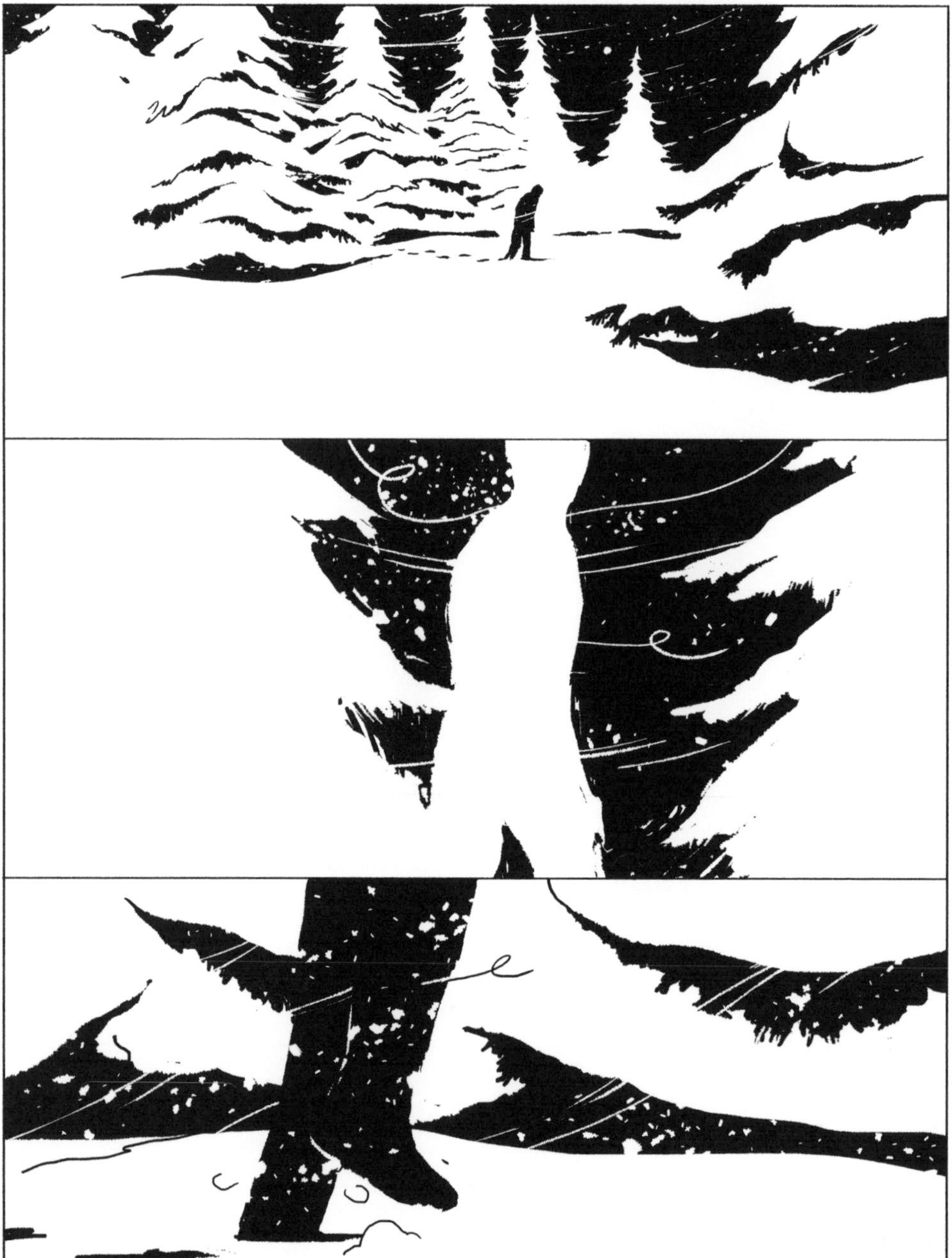

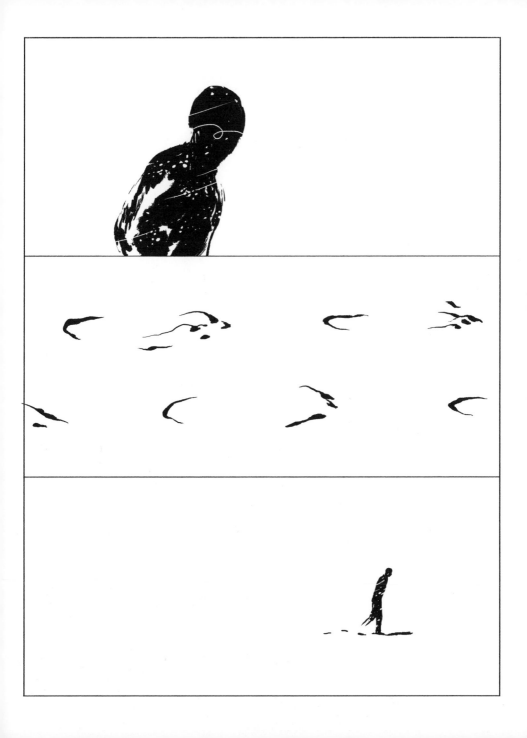

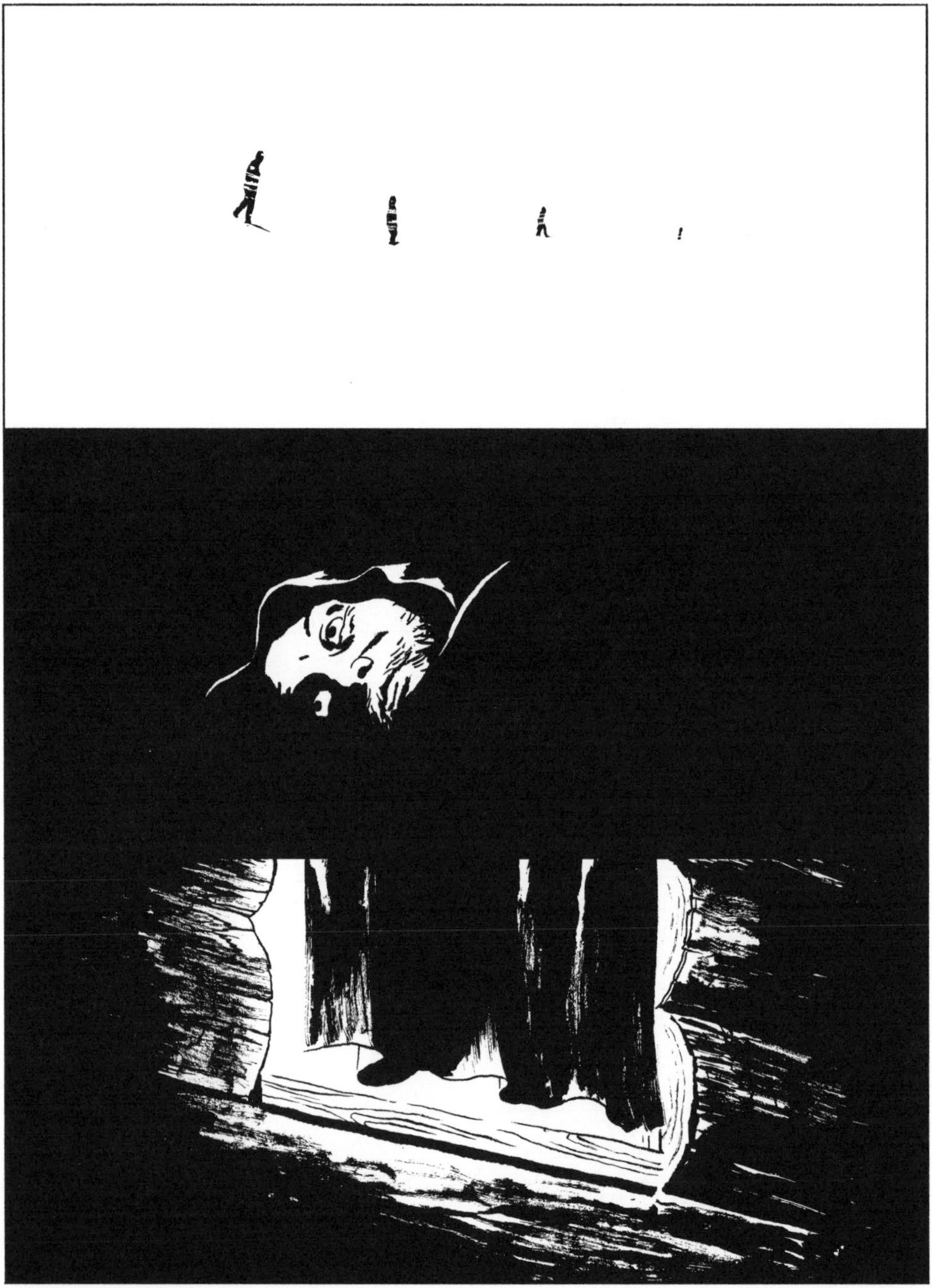

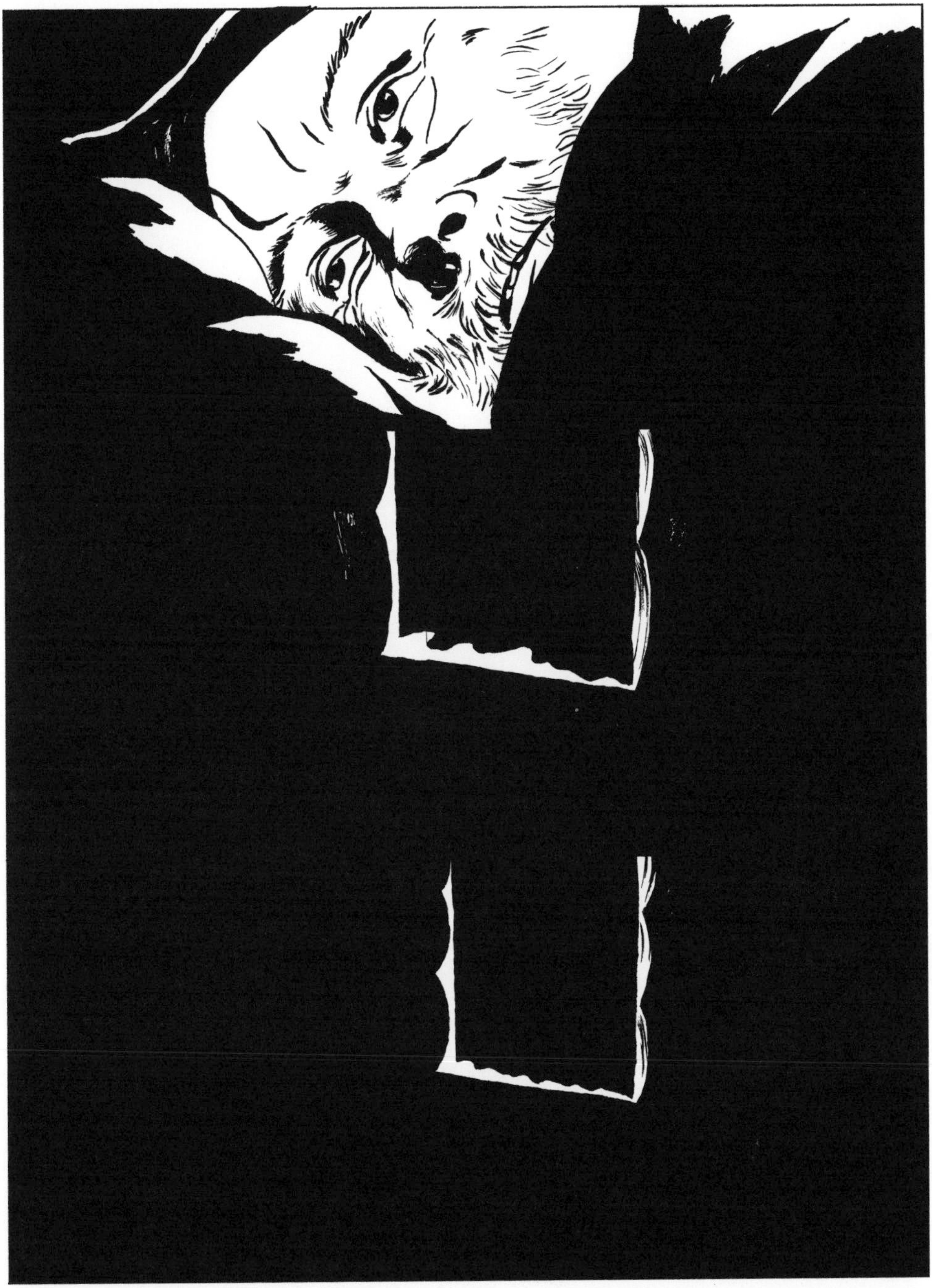

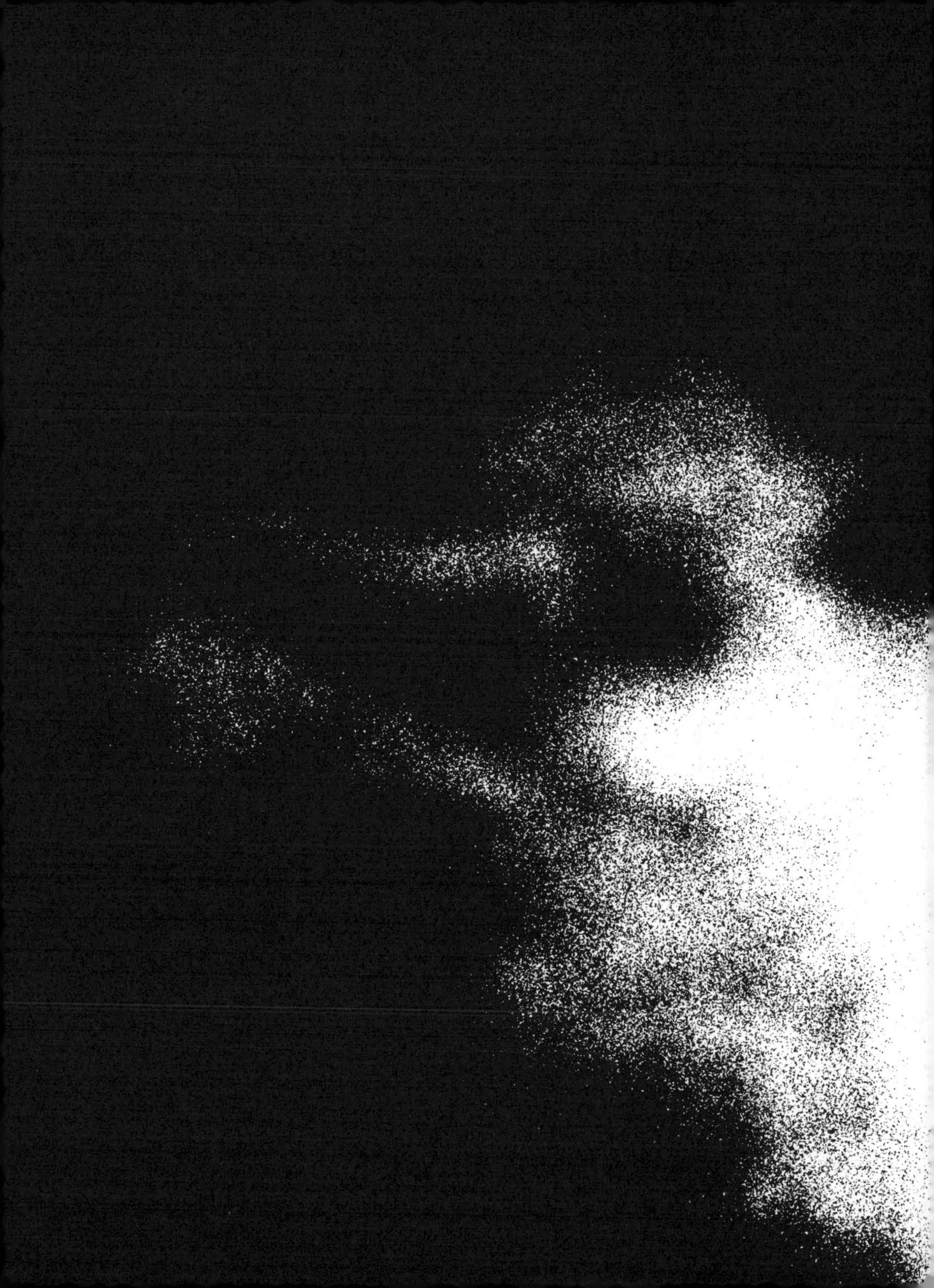

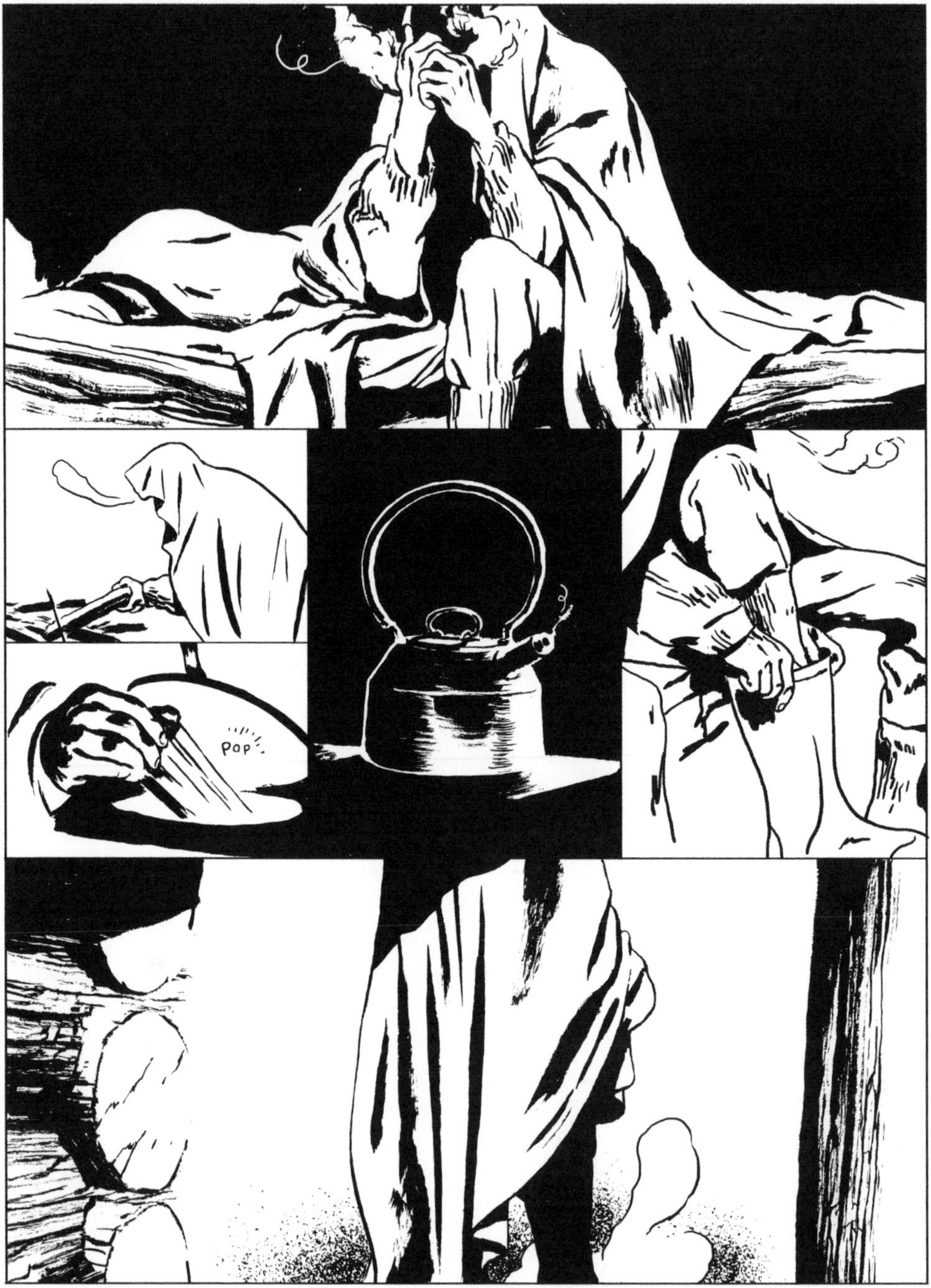
POP

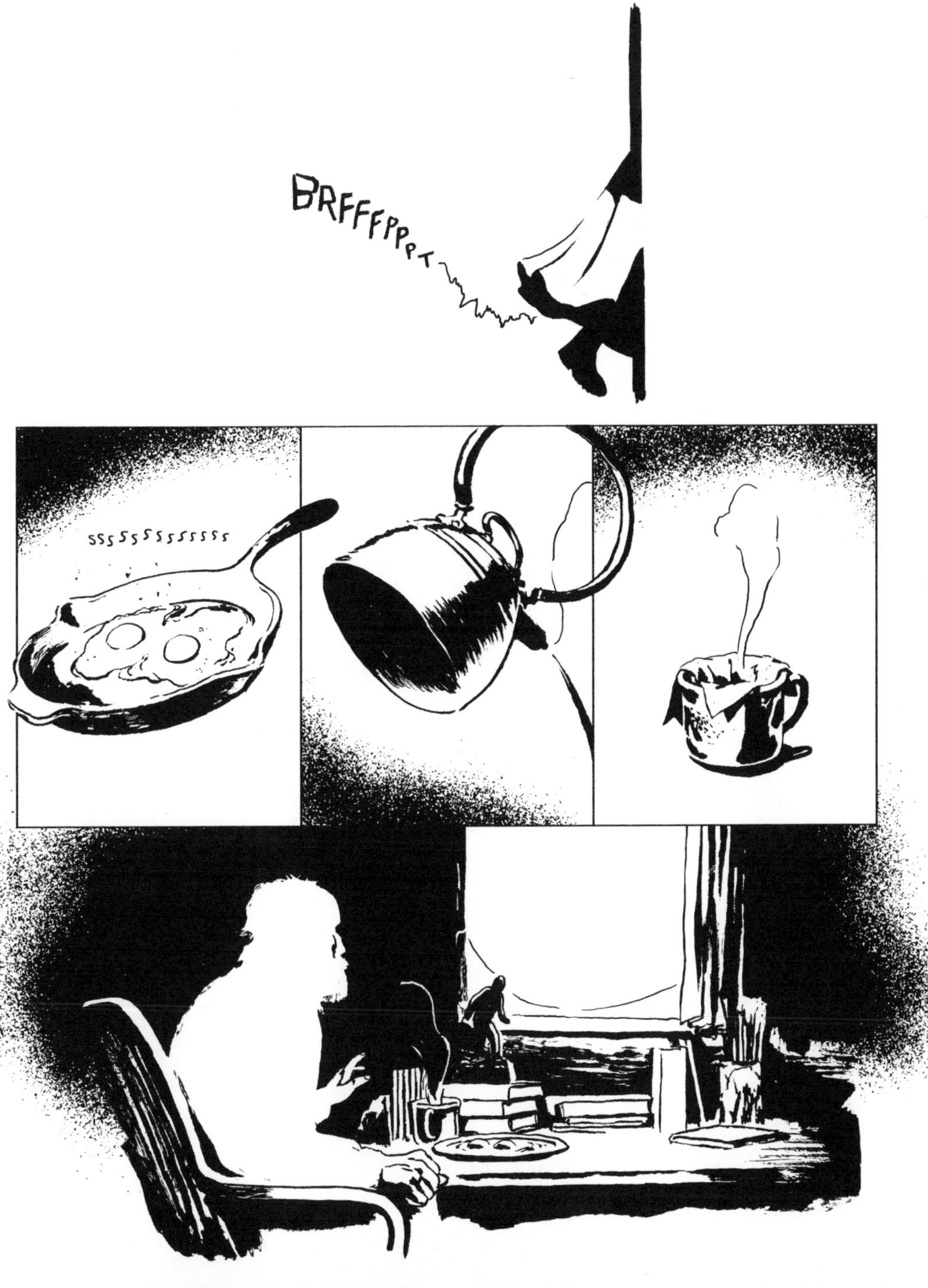
BRFFFPPPT
SSSSSSSSSSSSS

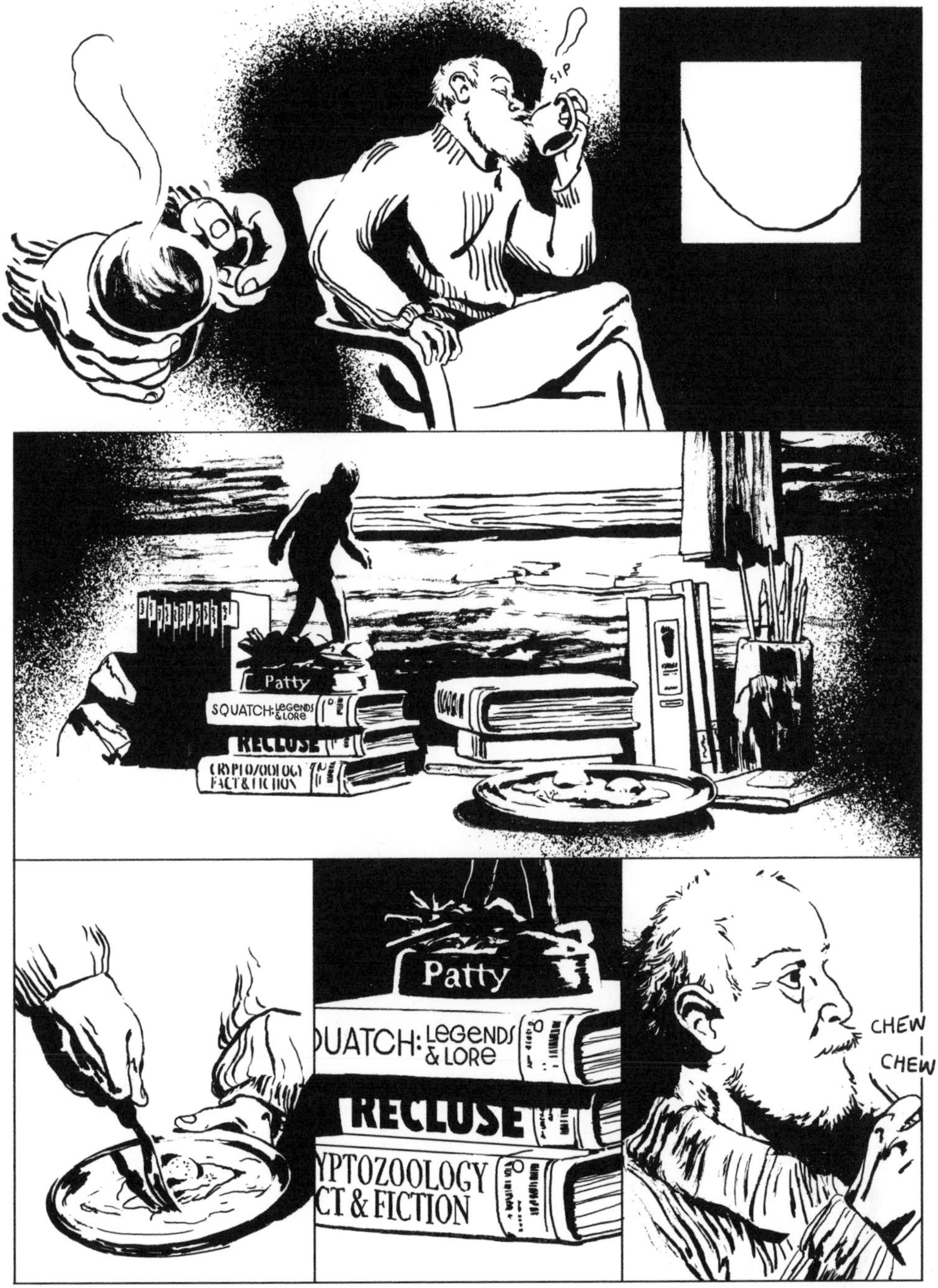
SIP
Patty
SQUATCH: LEGENDS & LORE
RECLUSE
CRYPTOZOOLOGY FACT & FICTION
Patty
UATCH: LEGENDS & LORE
RECLUSE
YPTOZOOLOGY
CT & FICTION
CHEW
CHEW

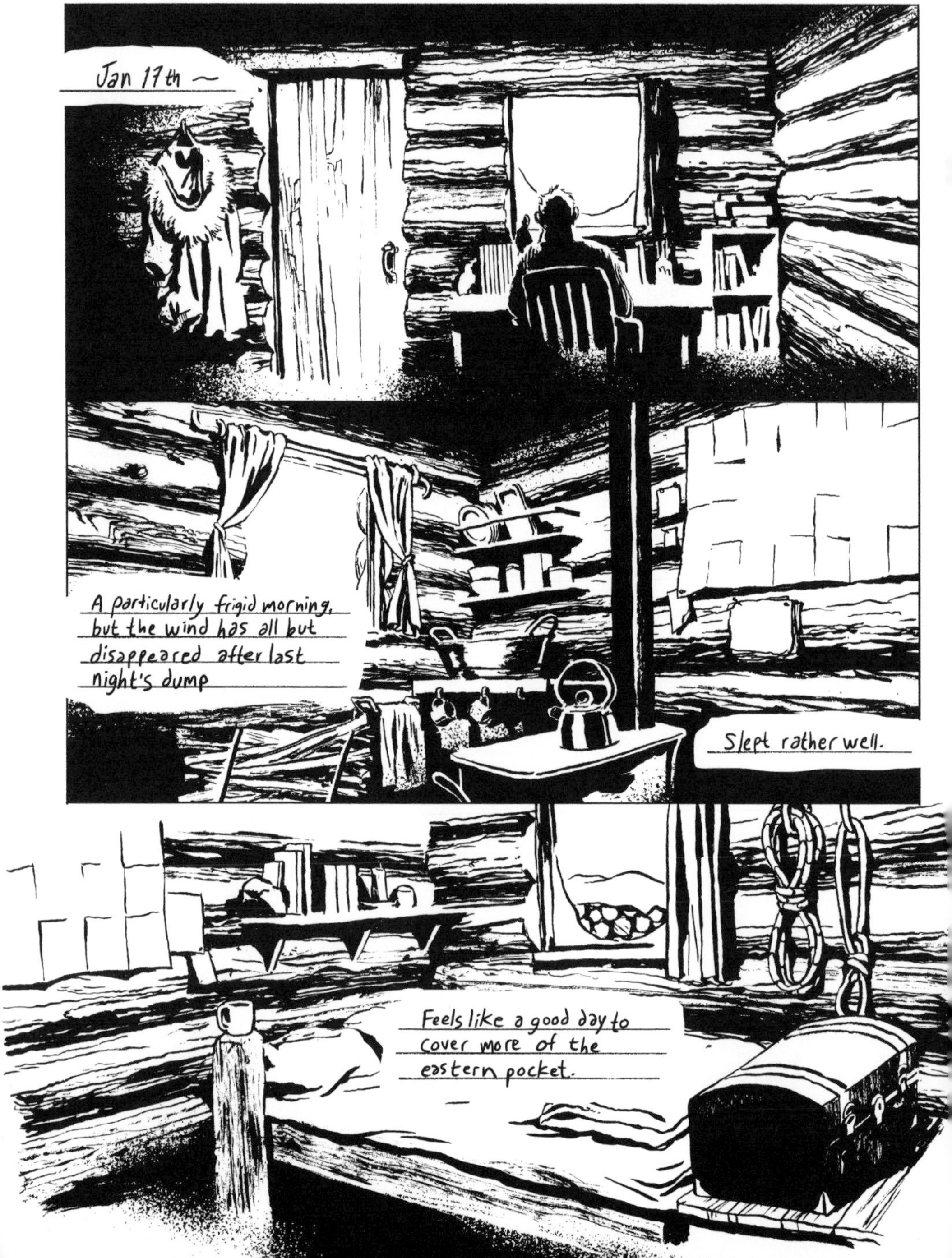
Jan 17th ~
A particularly frigid morning, but the wind has all but disappeared after last night's dump
Slept rather well.
Feels like a good day to cover more of the eastern pocket.

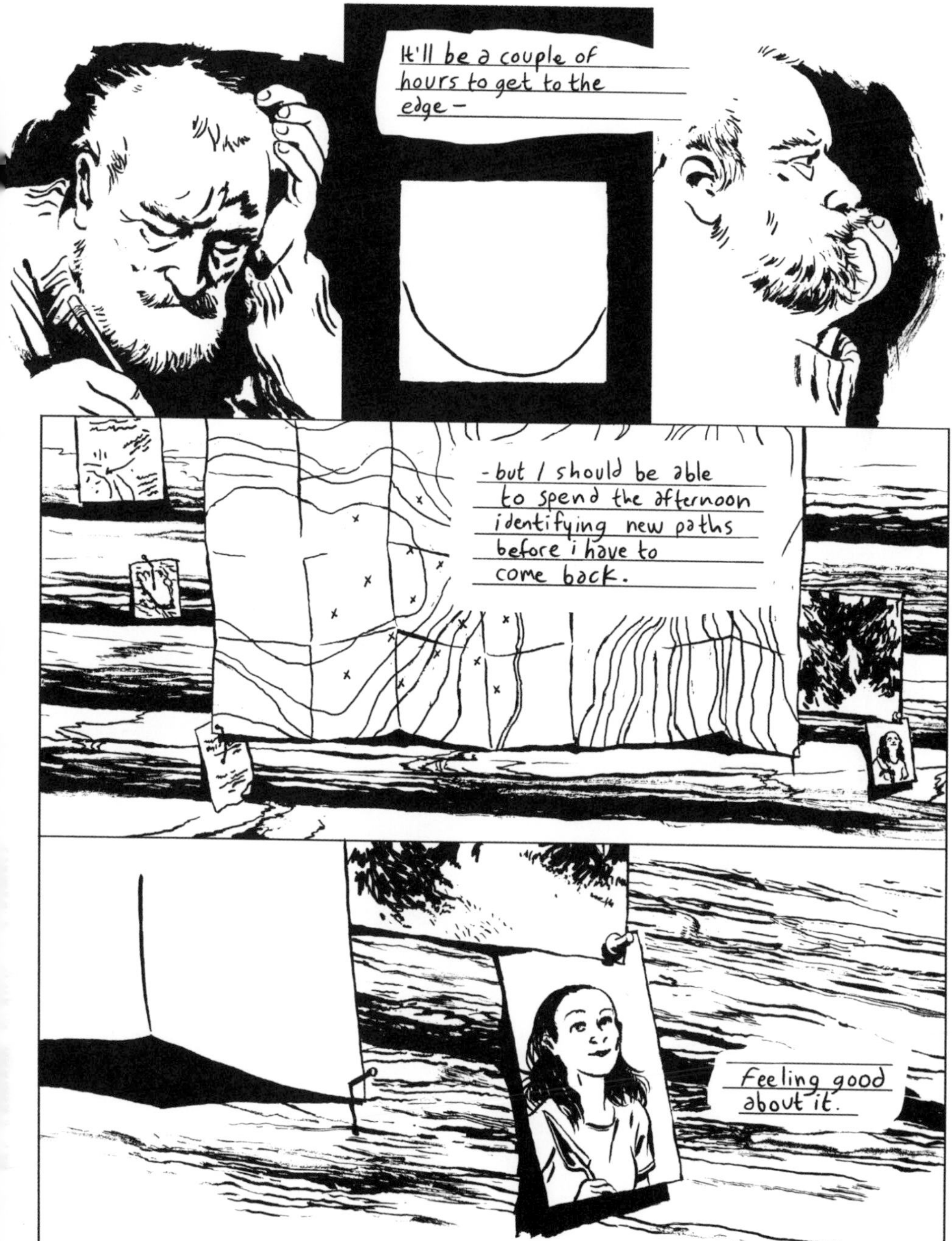
It'll be a couple of hours to get to the edge –
- but I should be able to spend the afternoon identifying new paths before i have to come back.
Feeling good about it.

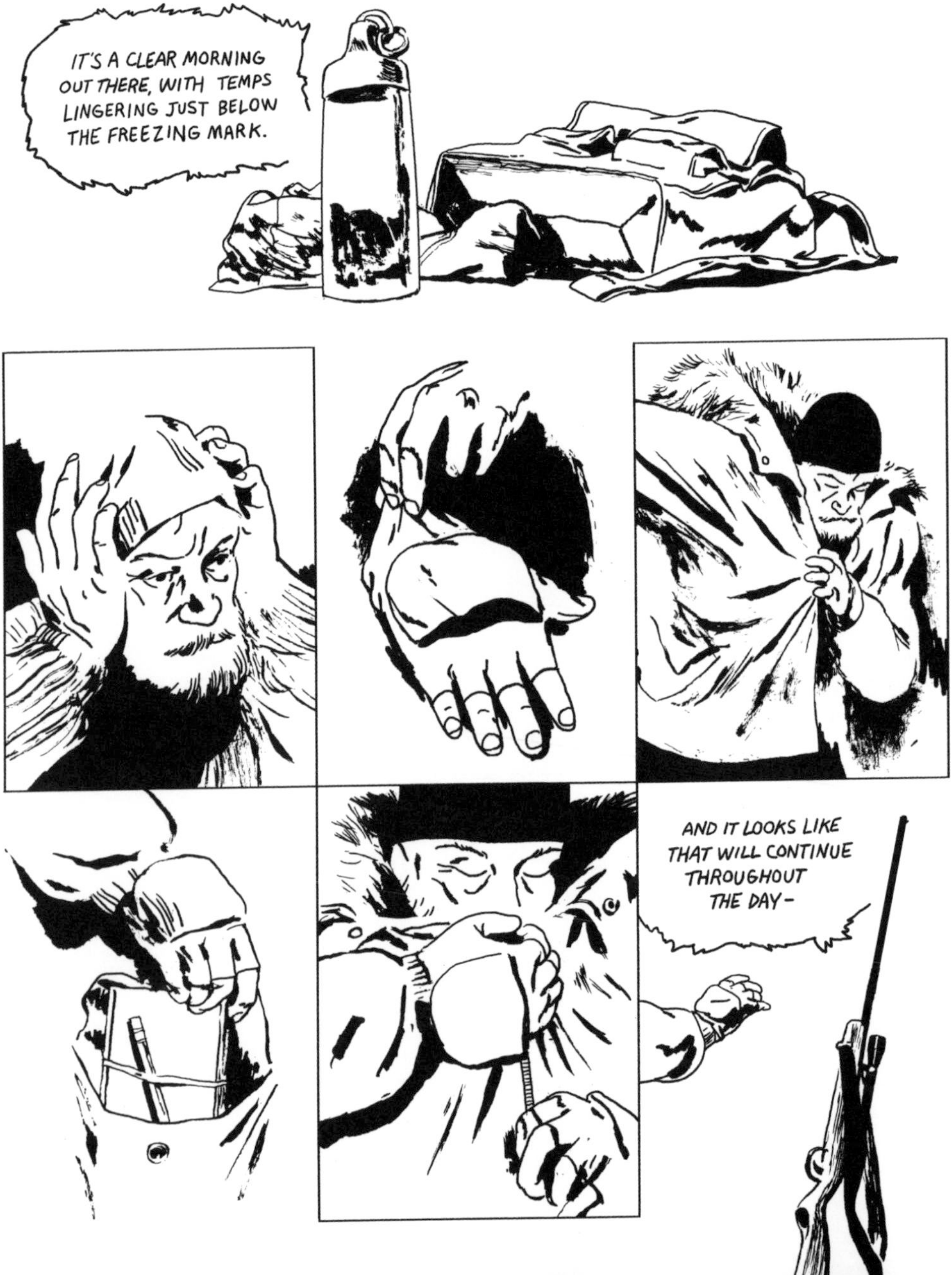
IT'S A CLEAR MORNING OUT THERE, WITH TEMPS LINGERING JUST BELOW THE FREEZING MARK.
AND IT LOOKS LIKE THAT WILL CONTINUE THROUGHOUT THE DAY-

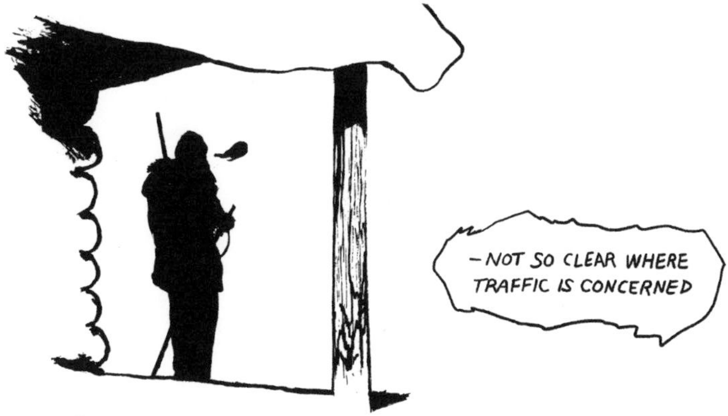
–NOT SO CLEAR WHERE TRAFFIC IS CONCERNED

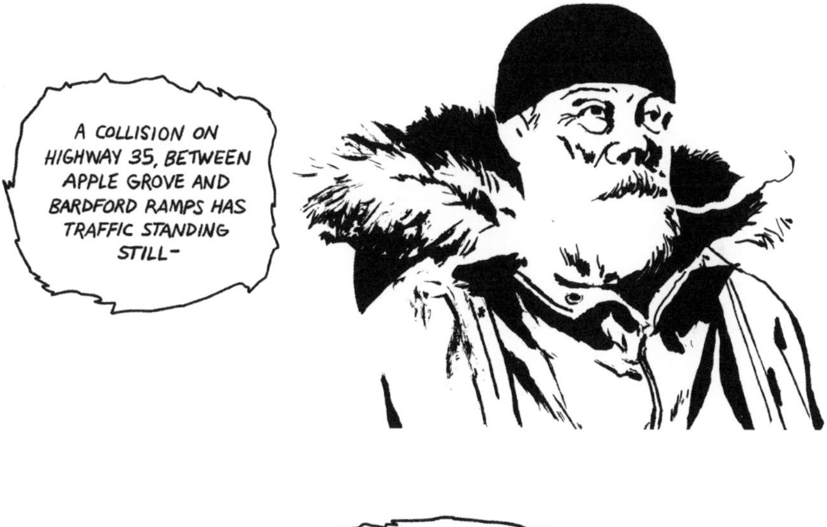
A COLLISION ON HIGHWAY 35, BETWEEN APPLE GROVE AND BARDFORD RAMPS HAS TRAFFIC STANDING STILL–

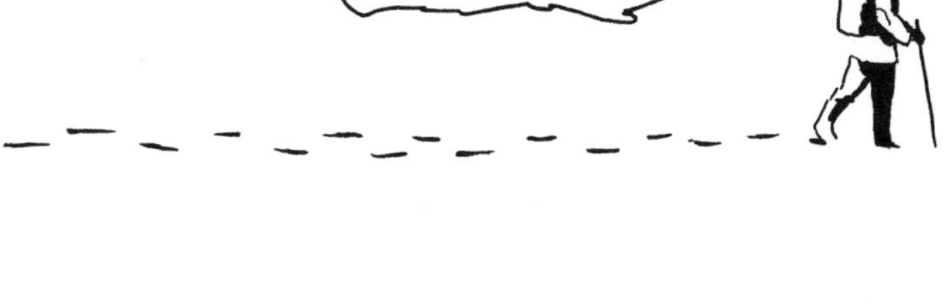
–WHILE EMERGENCY RESPONDERS WORK TO CLEAR THINGS UP

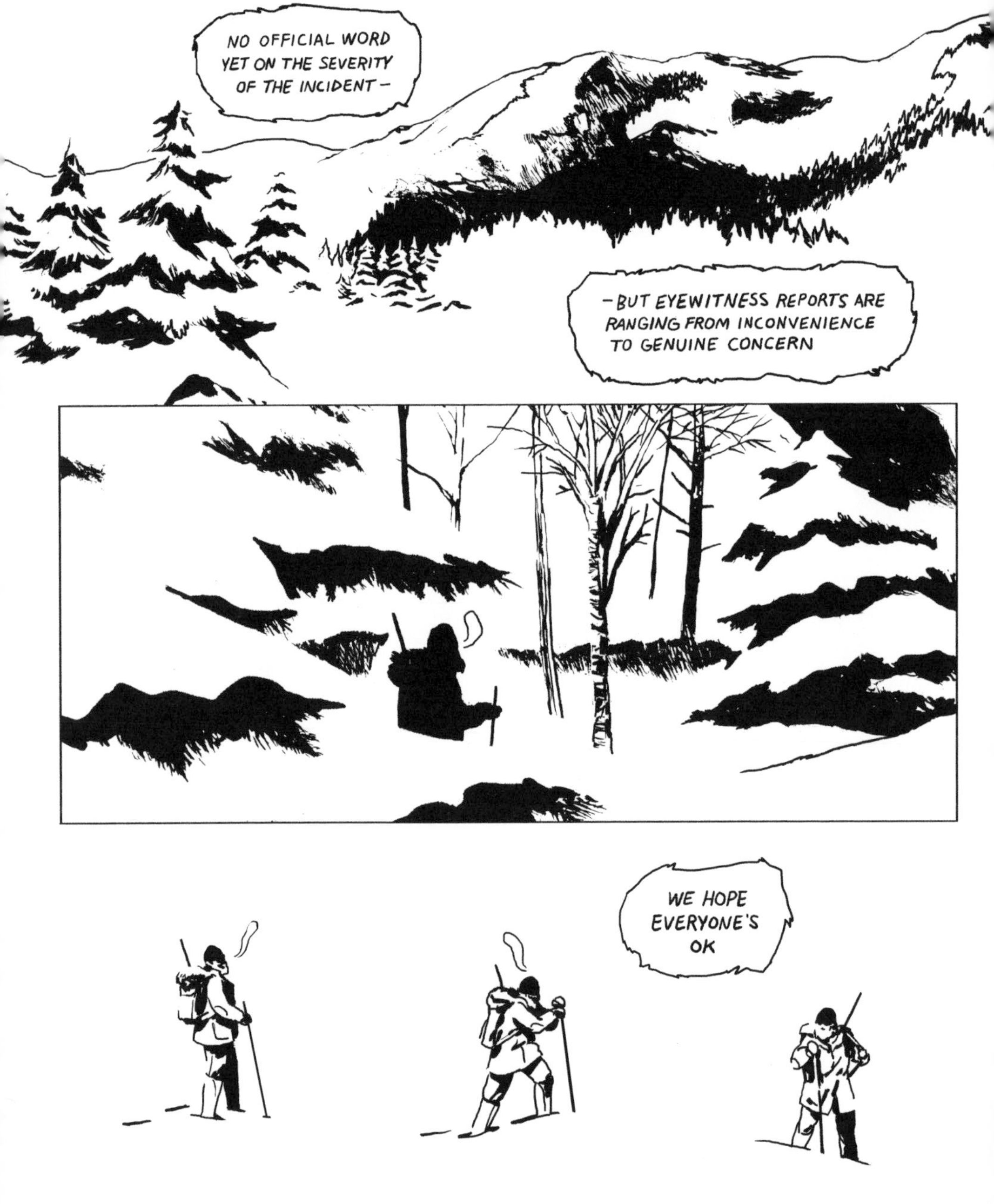
NO OFFICIAL WORD YET ON THE SEVERITY OF THE INCIDENT –
– BUT EYEWITNESS REPORTS ARE RANGING FROM INCONVENIENCE TO GENUINE CONCERN
WE HOPE EVERYONE'S OK

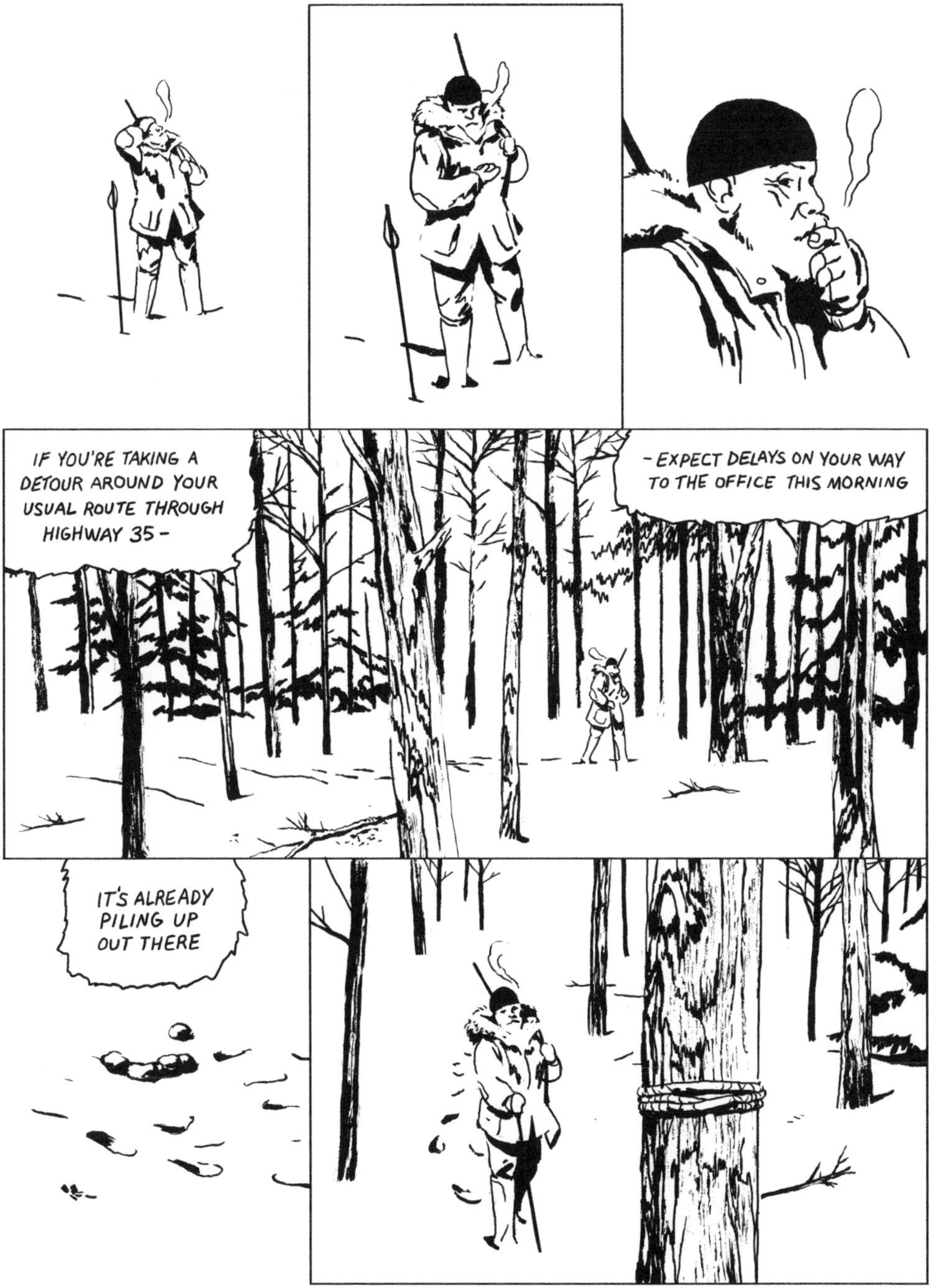
IF YOU'RE TAKING A DETOUR AROUND YOUR USUAL ROUTE THROUGH HIGHWAY 35 –
– EXPECT DELAYS ON YOUR WAY TO THE OFFICE THIS MORNING
IT'S ALREADY PILING UP OUT THERE

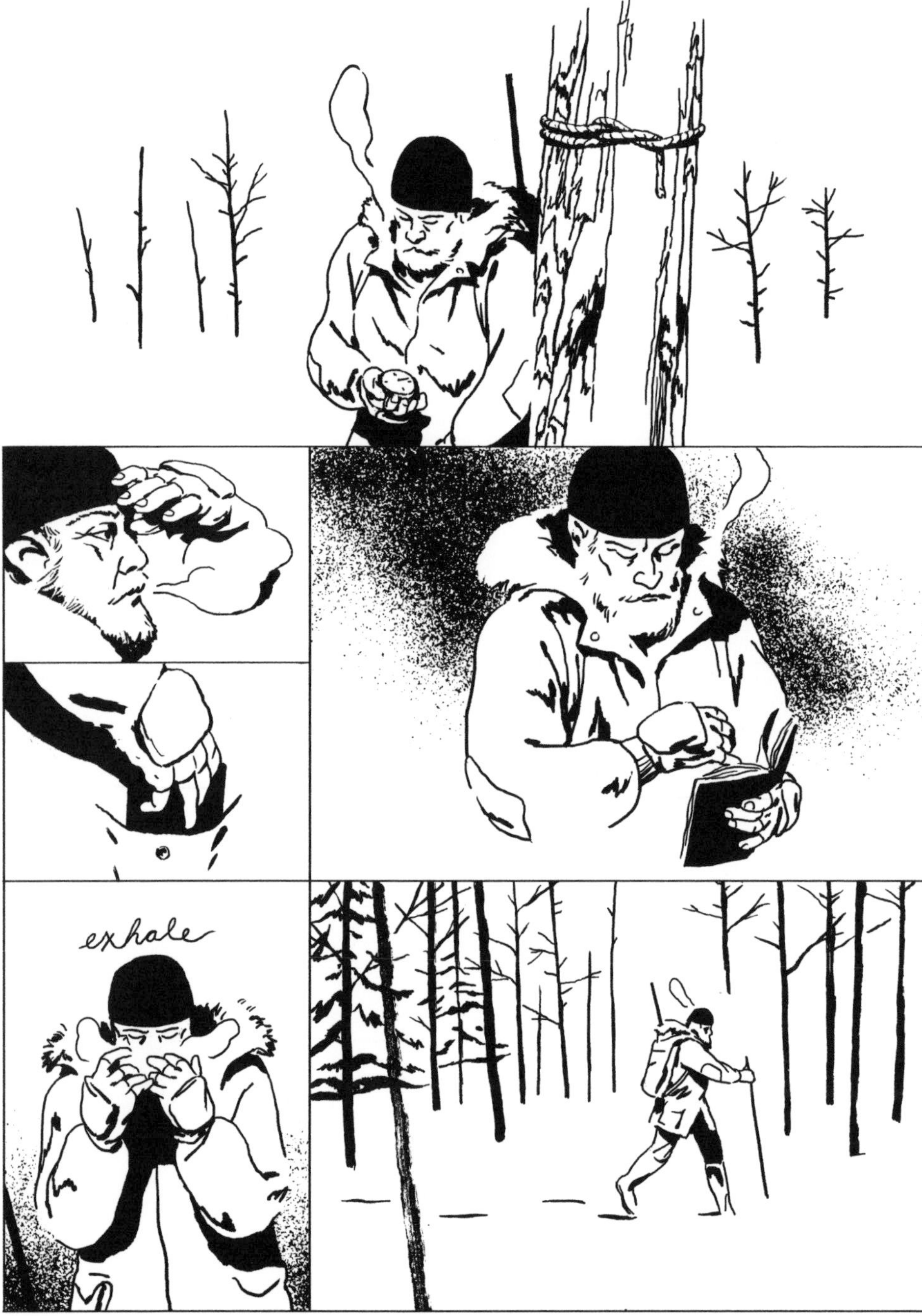
exhale

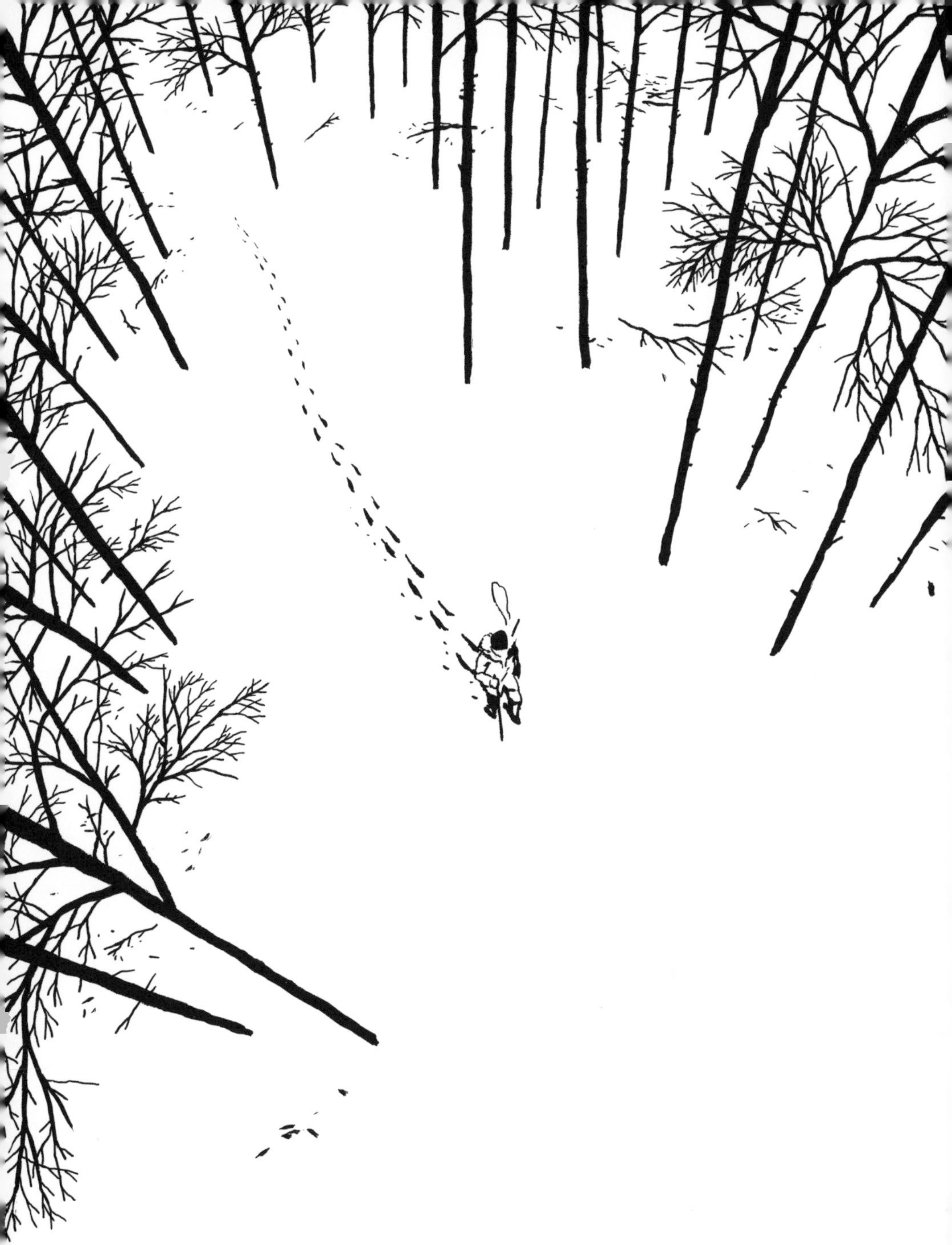

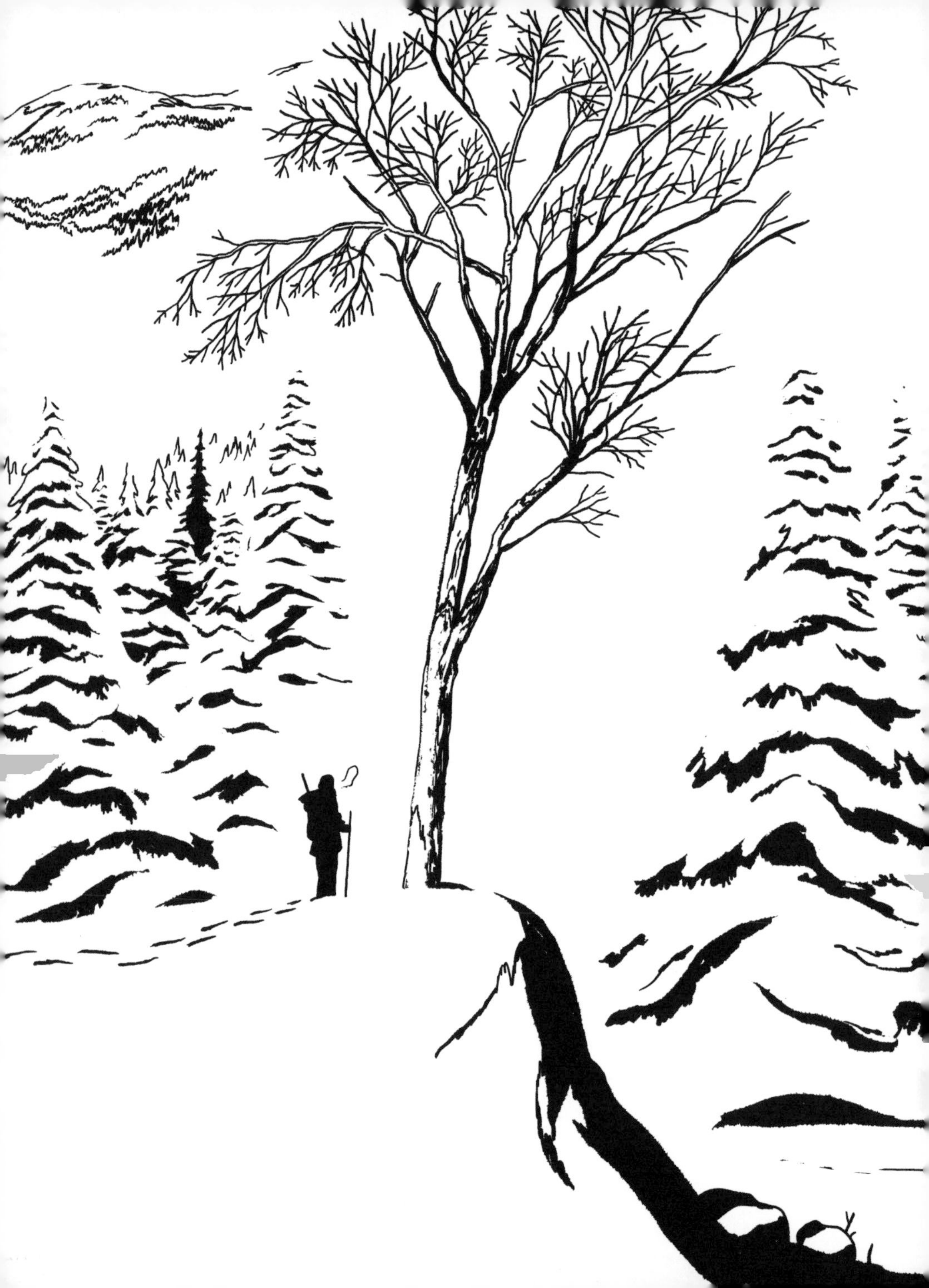

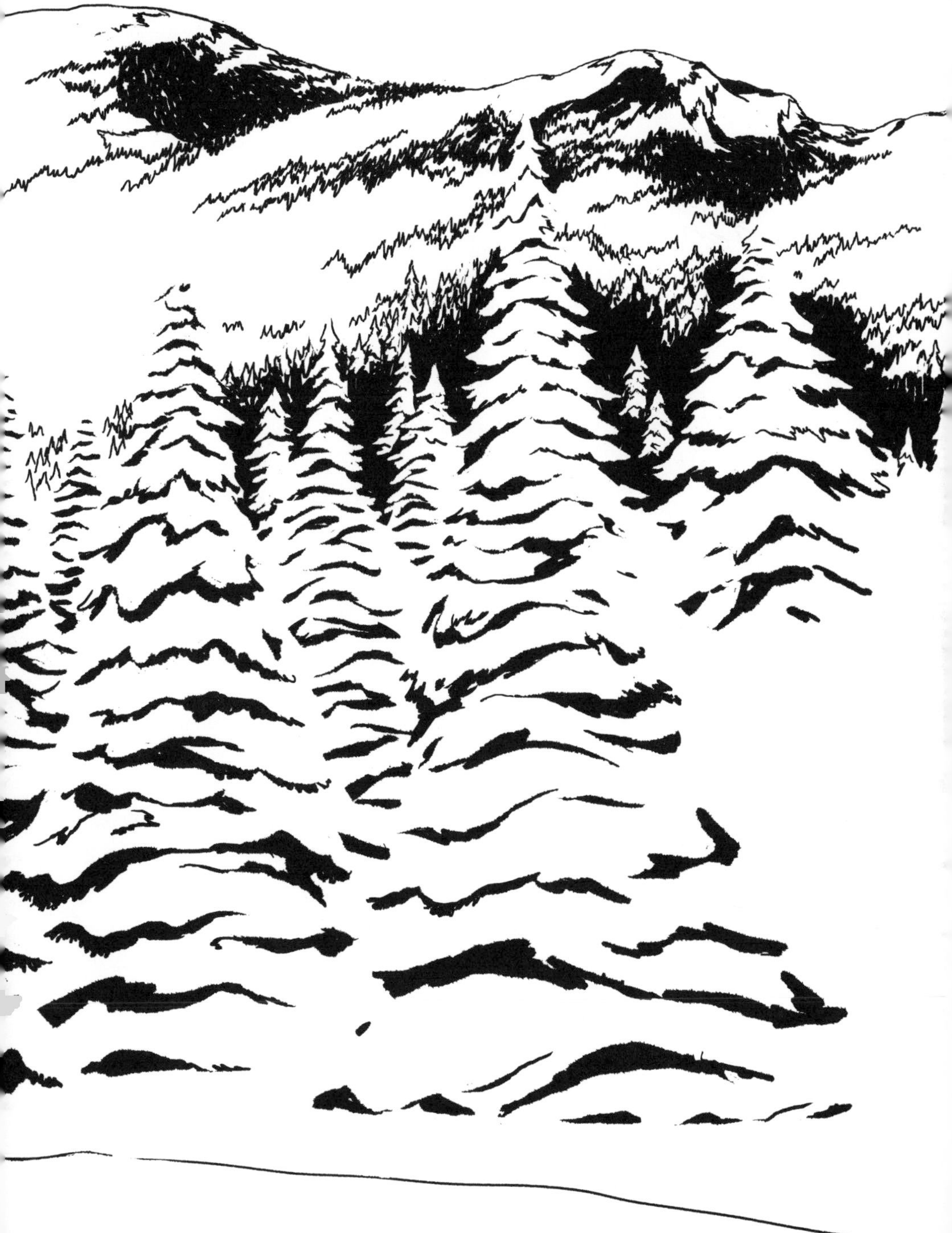

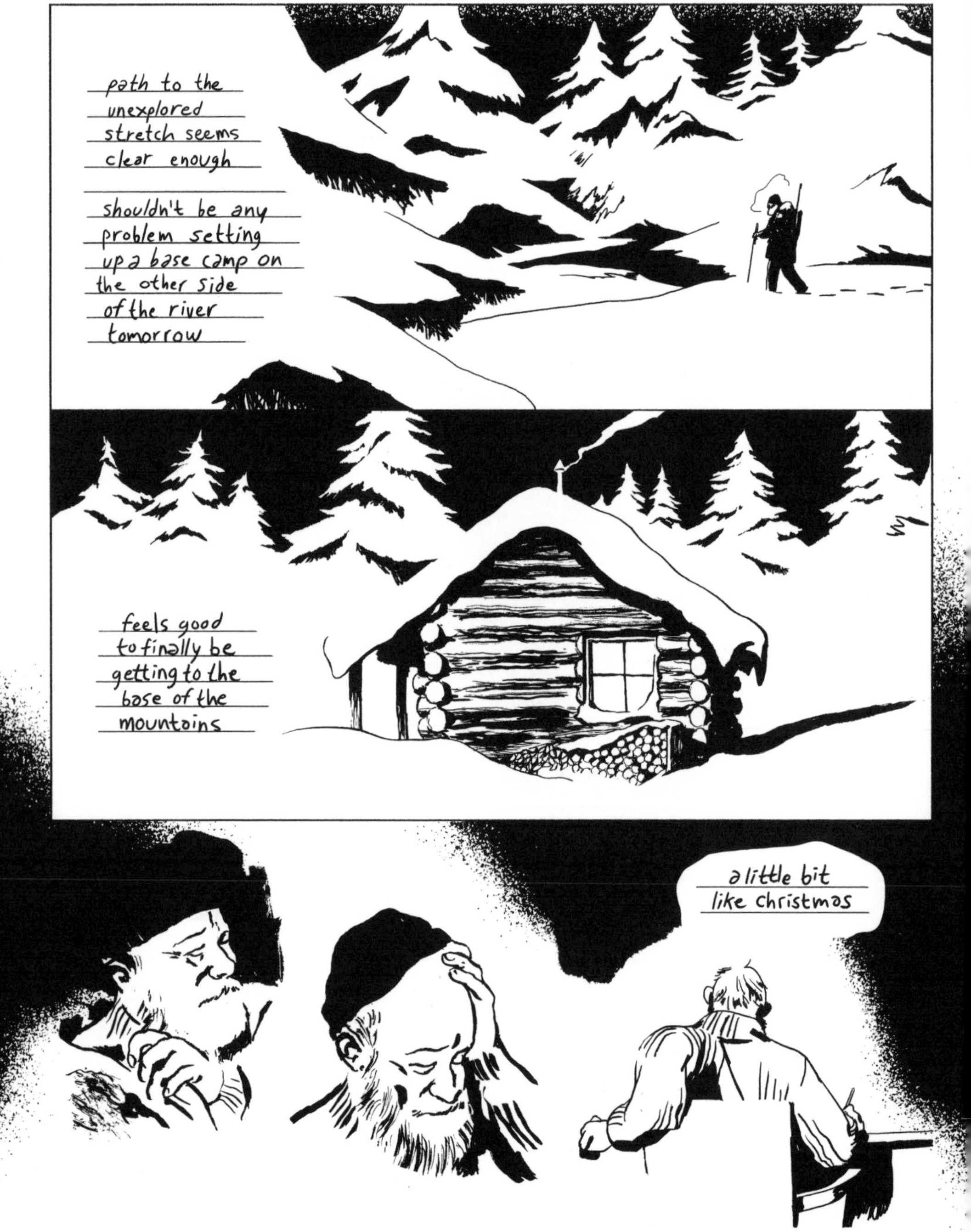
path to the unexplored stretch seems clear enough
shouldn't be any problem setting up a base camp on the other side of the river tomorrow
feels good to finally be getting to the base of the mountains
a little bit like christmas

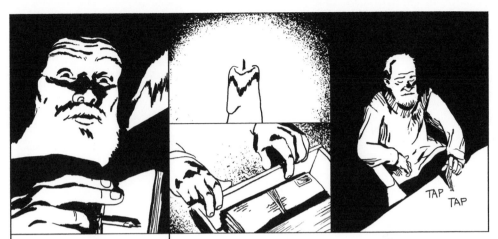

TAP

TAP

TAP TAP

ZZZZ

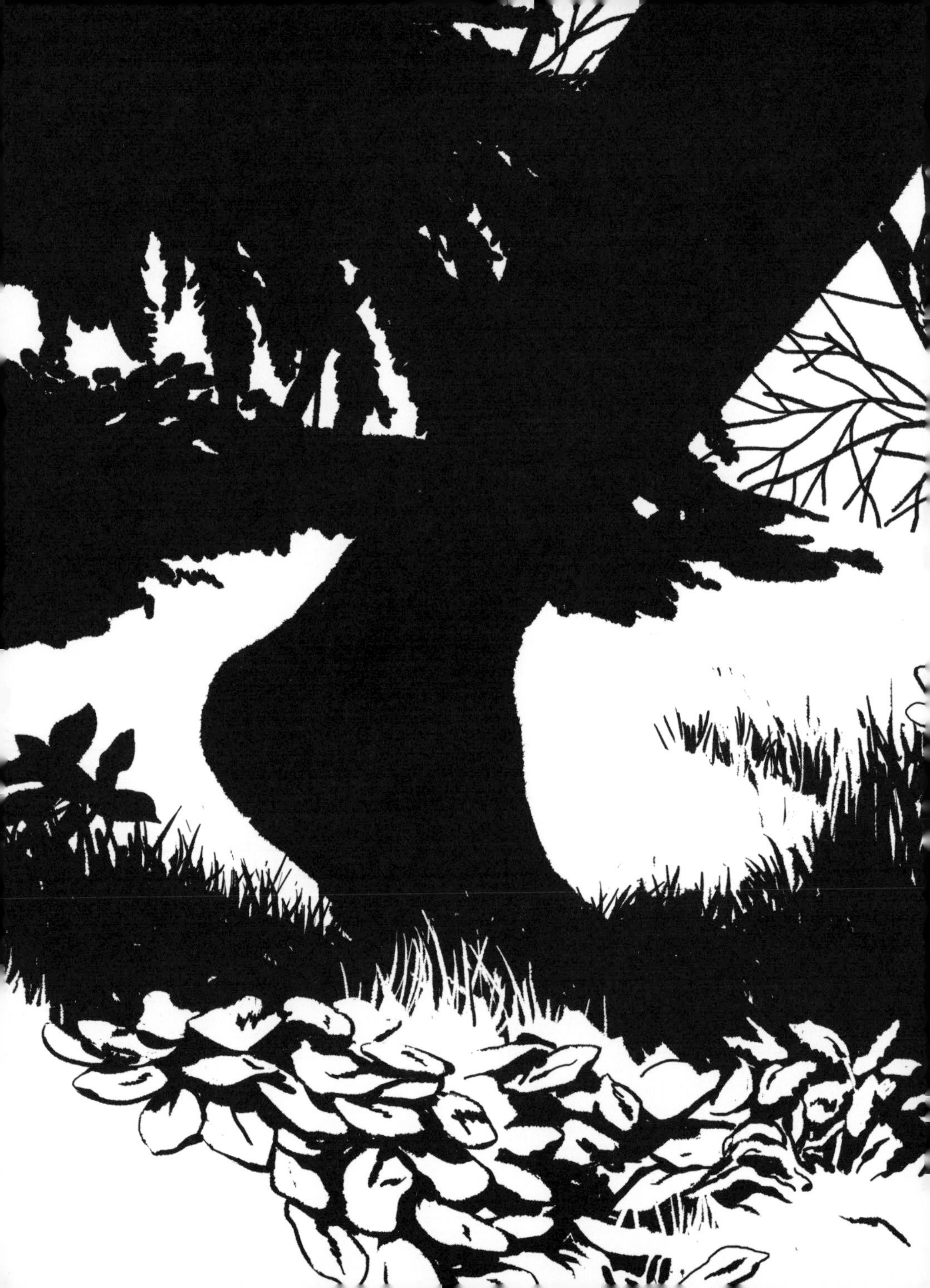

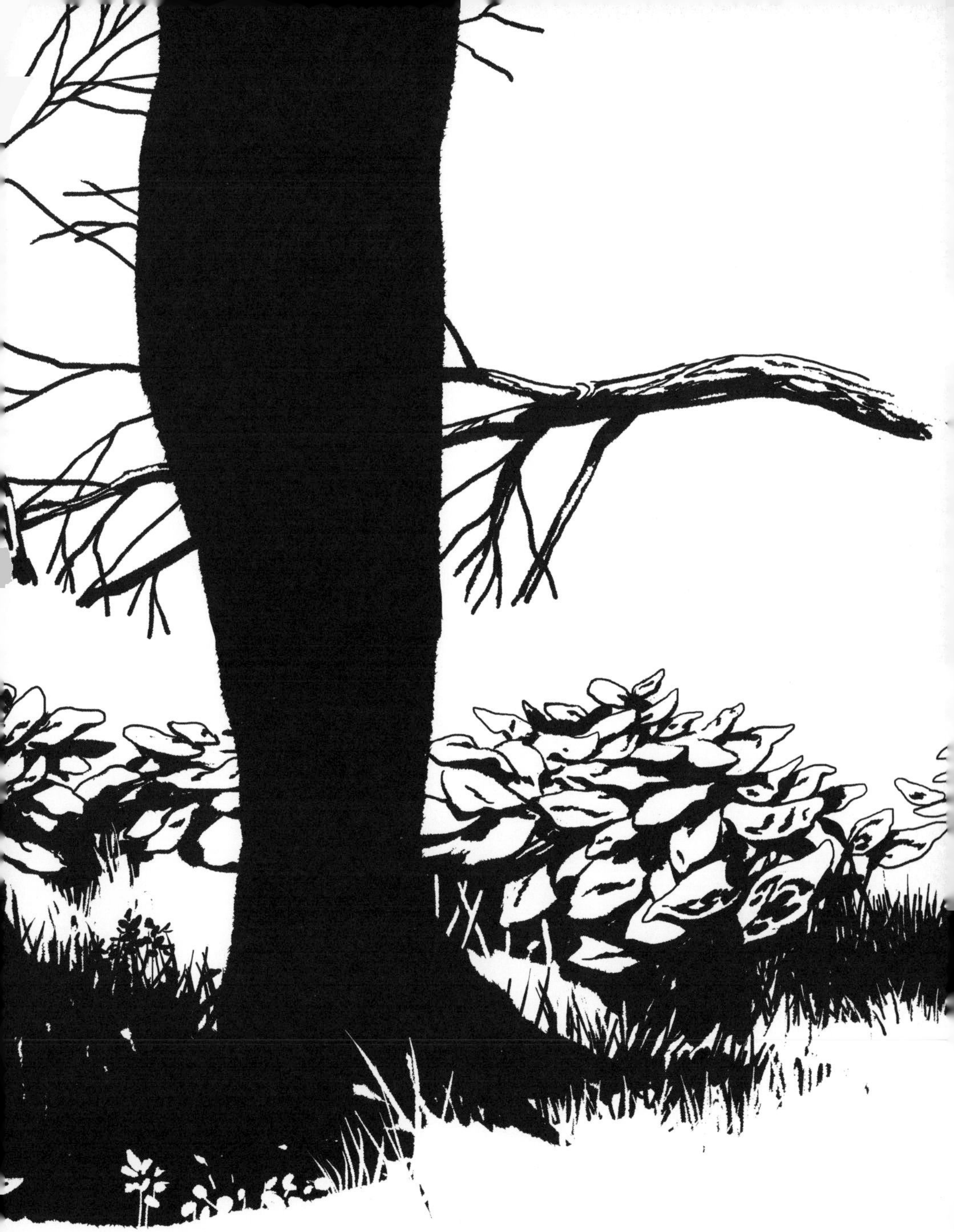

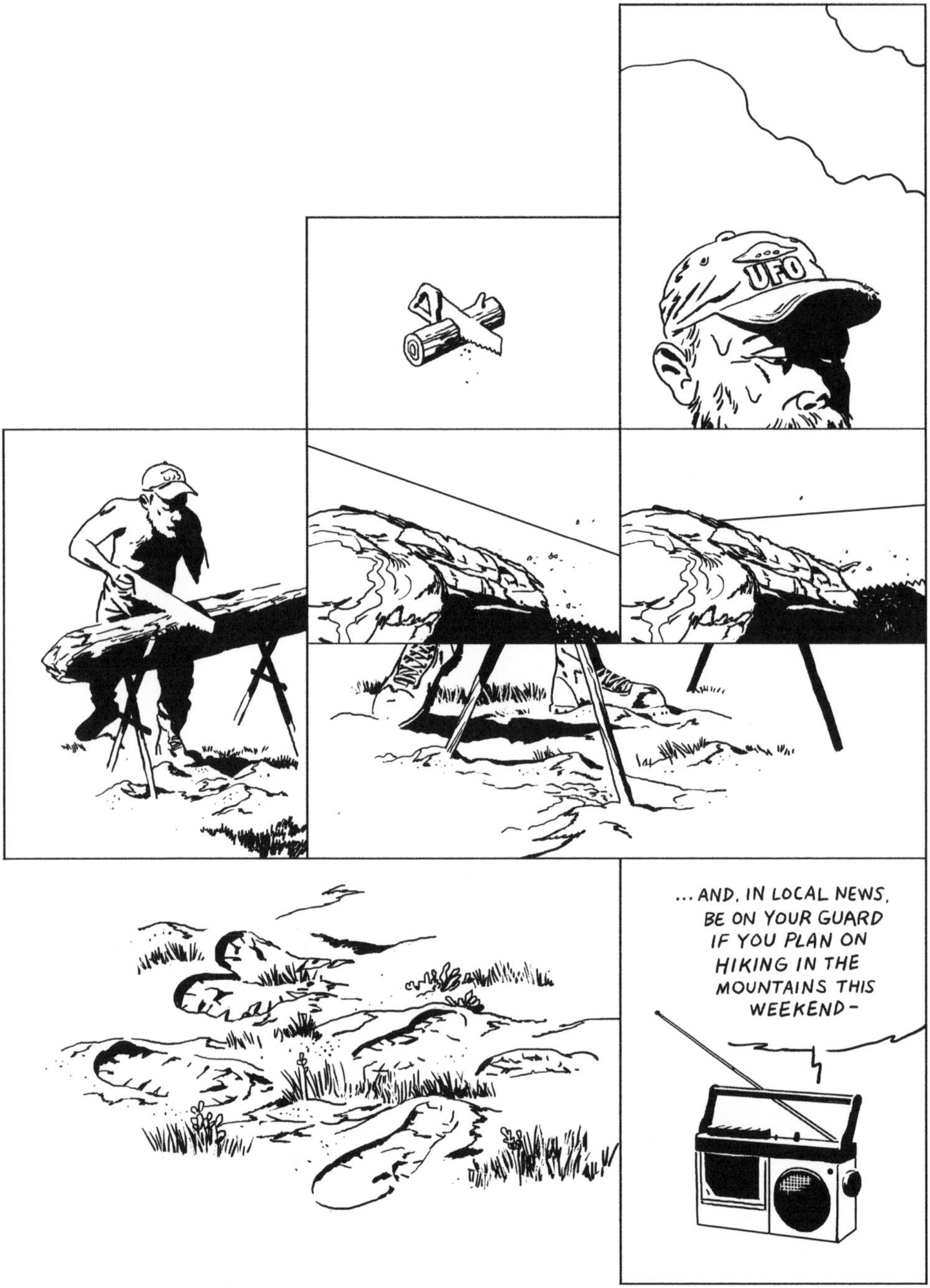
UFO
... AND, IN LOCAL NEWS, BE ON YOUR GUARD IF YOU PLAN ON HIKING IN THE MOUNTAINS THIS WEEKEND-

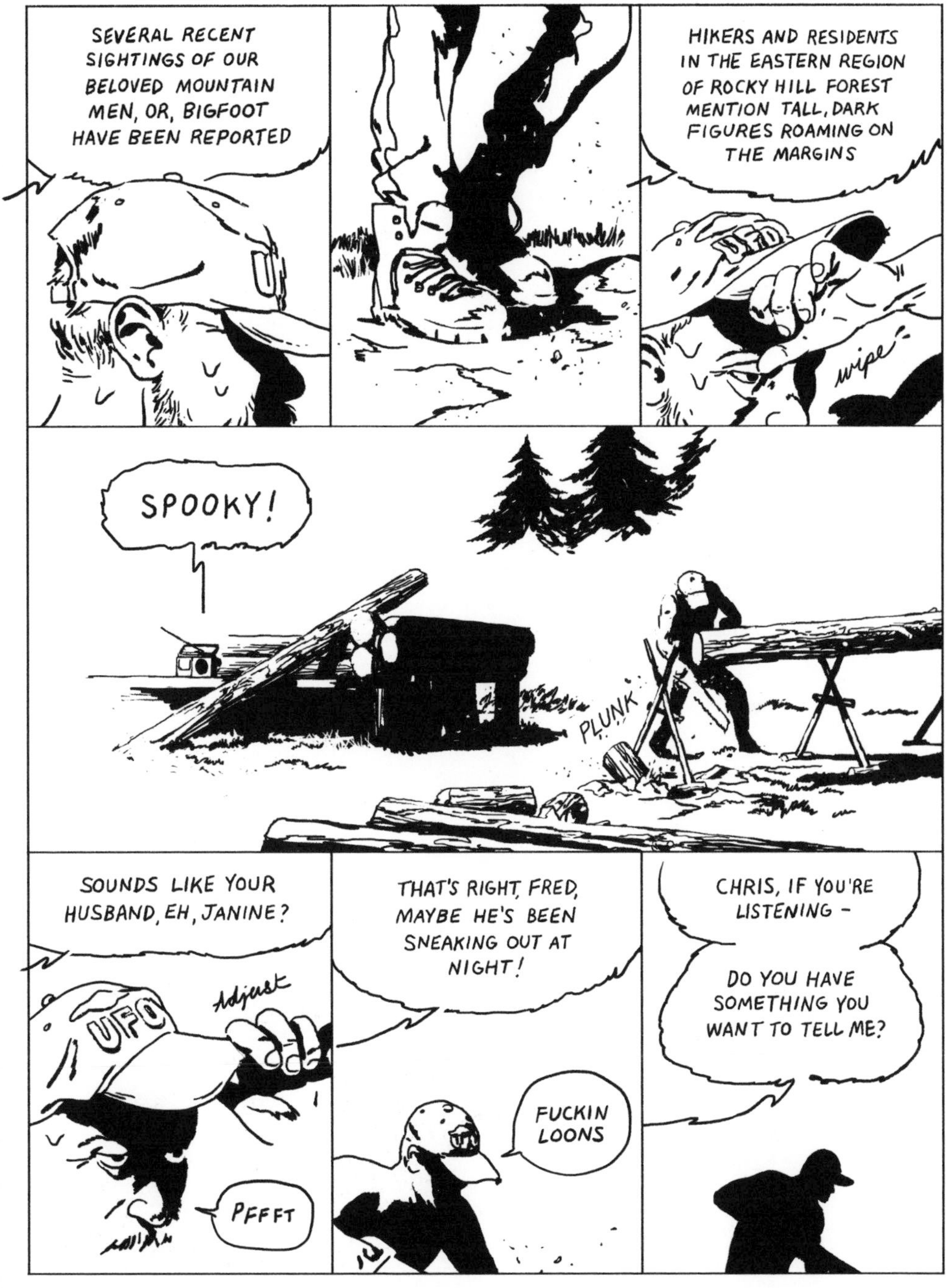
SEVERAL RECENT SIGHTINGS OF OUR BELOVED MOUNTAIN MEN, OR, BIGFOOT HAVE BEEN REPORTED
HIKERS AND RESIDENTS IN THE EASTERN REGION OF ROCKY HILL FOREST MENTION TALL, DARK FIGURES ROAMING ON THE MARGINS
wipe
SPOOKY!
PLUNK
SOUNDS LIKE YOUR HUSBAND, EH, JANINE?
Adjust
UFO
PFFFT
THAT'S RIGHT, FRED, MAYBE HE'S BEEN SNEAKING OUT AT NIGHT!
FUCKIN LOONS
CHRIS, IF YOU'RE LISTENING -
DO YOU HAVE SOMETHING YOU WANT TO TELL ME?

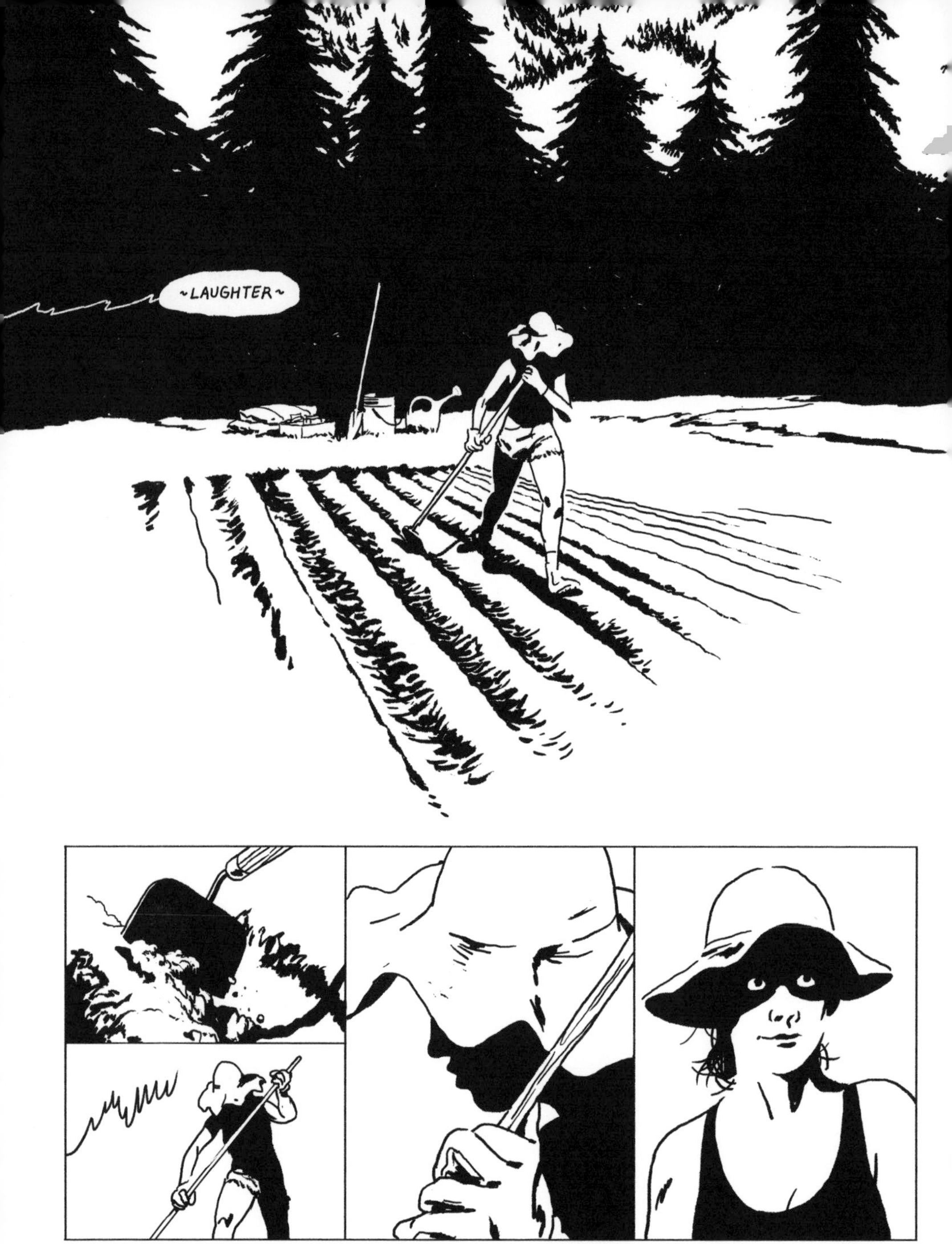
~LAUGHTER~

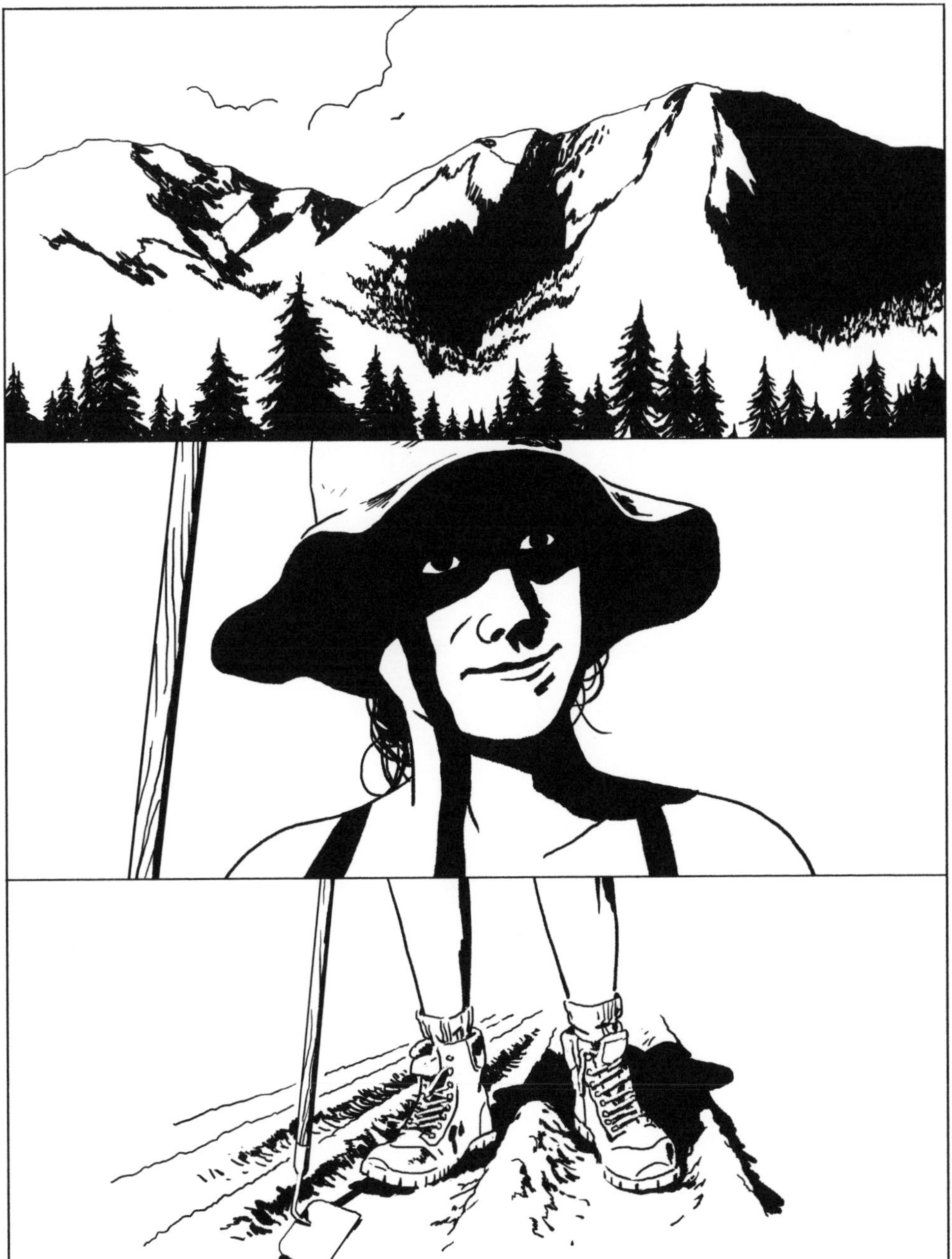

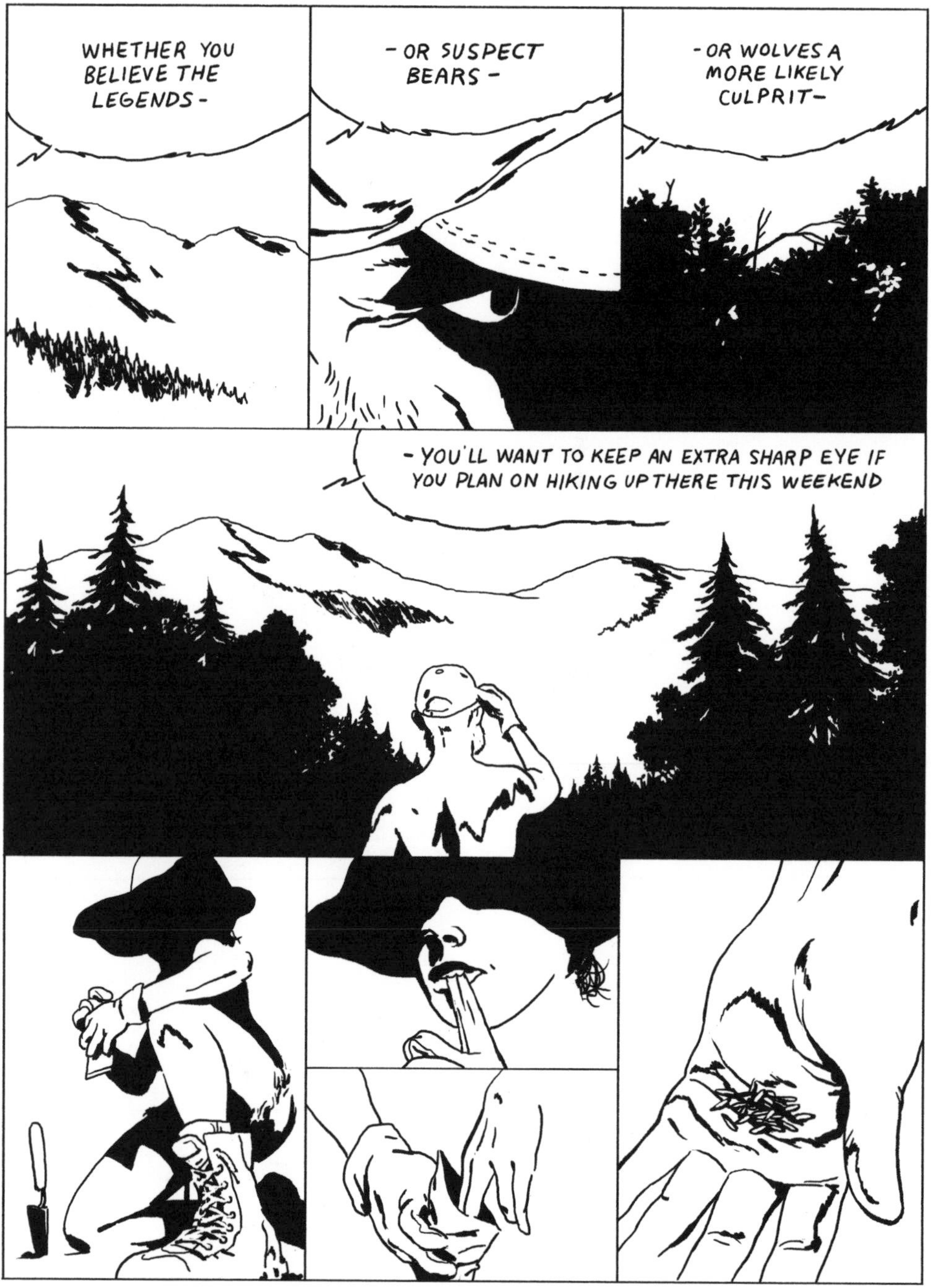
WHETHER YOU BELIEVE THE LEGENDS-
-OR SUSPECT BEARS-
-OR WOLVES A MORE LIKELY CULPRIT-
-YOU'LL WANT TO KEEP AN EXTRA SHARP EYE IF YOU PLAN ON HIKING UP THERE THIS WEEKEND

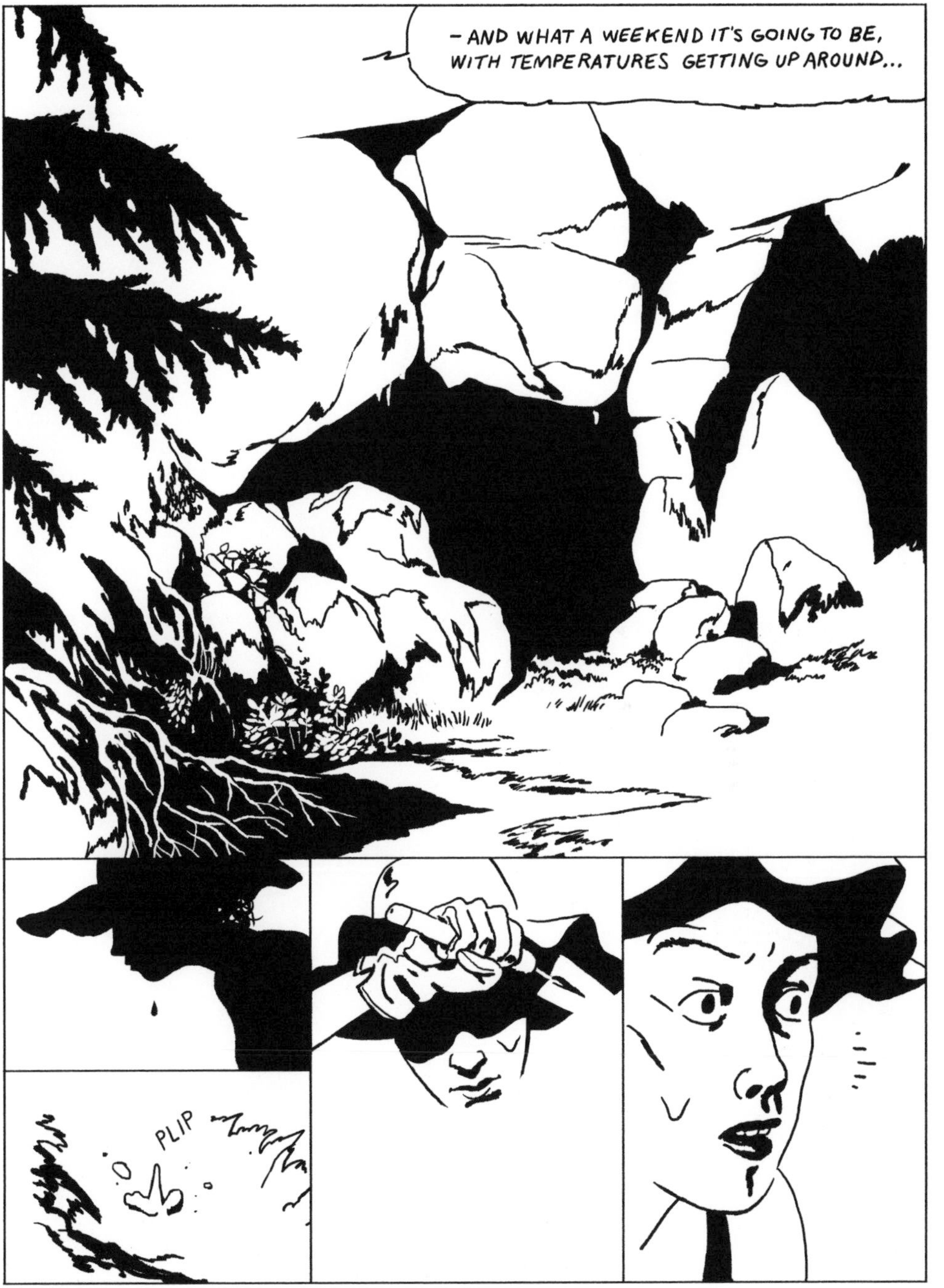
– AND WHAT A WEEKEND IT'S GOING TO BE, WITH TEMPERATURES GETTING UP AROUND...
PLIP

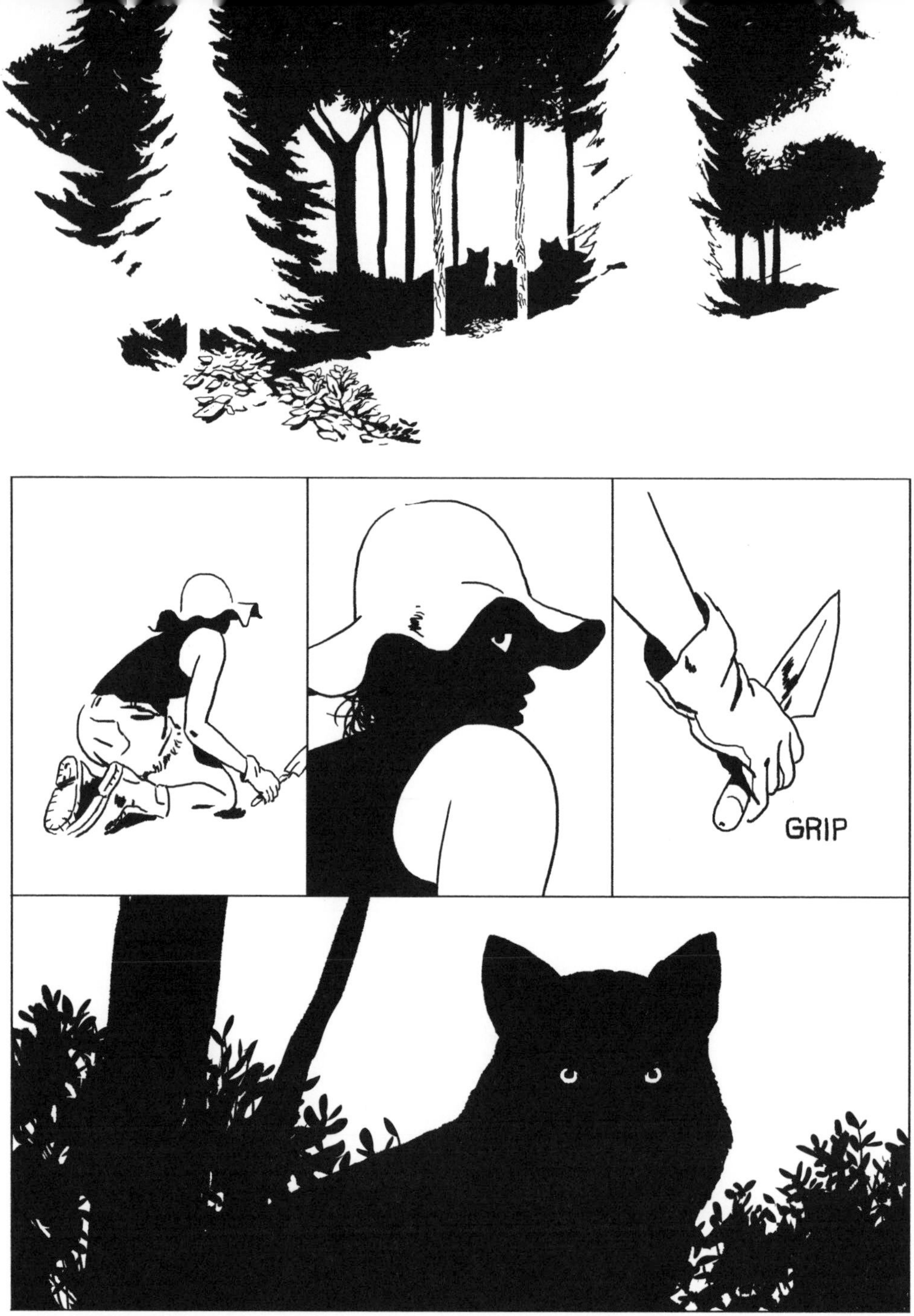
GRIP

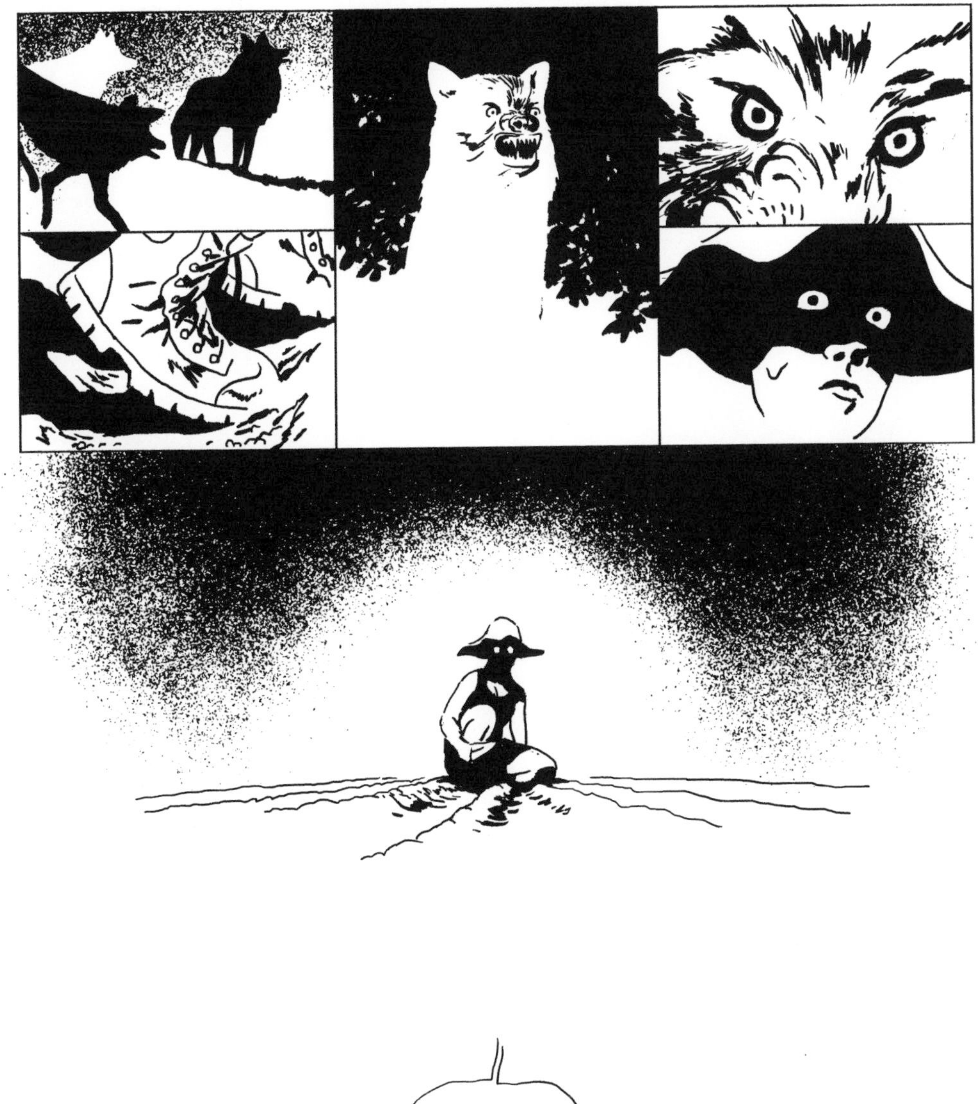
HONEY?

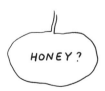

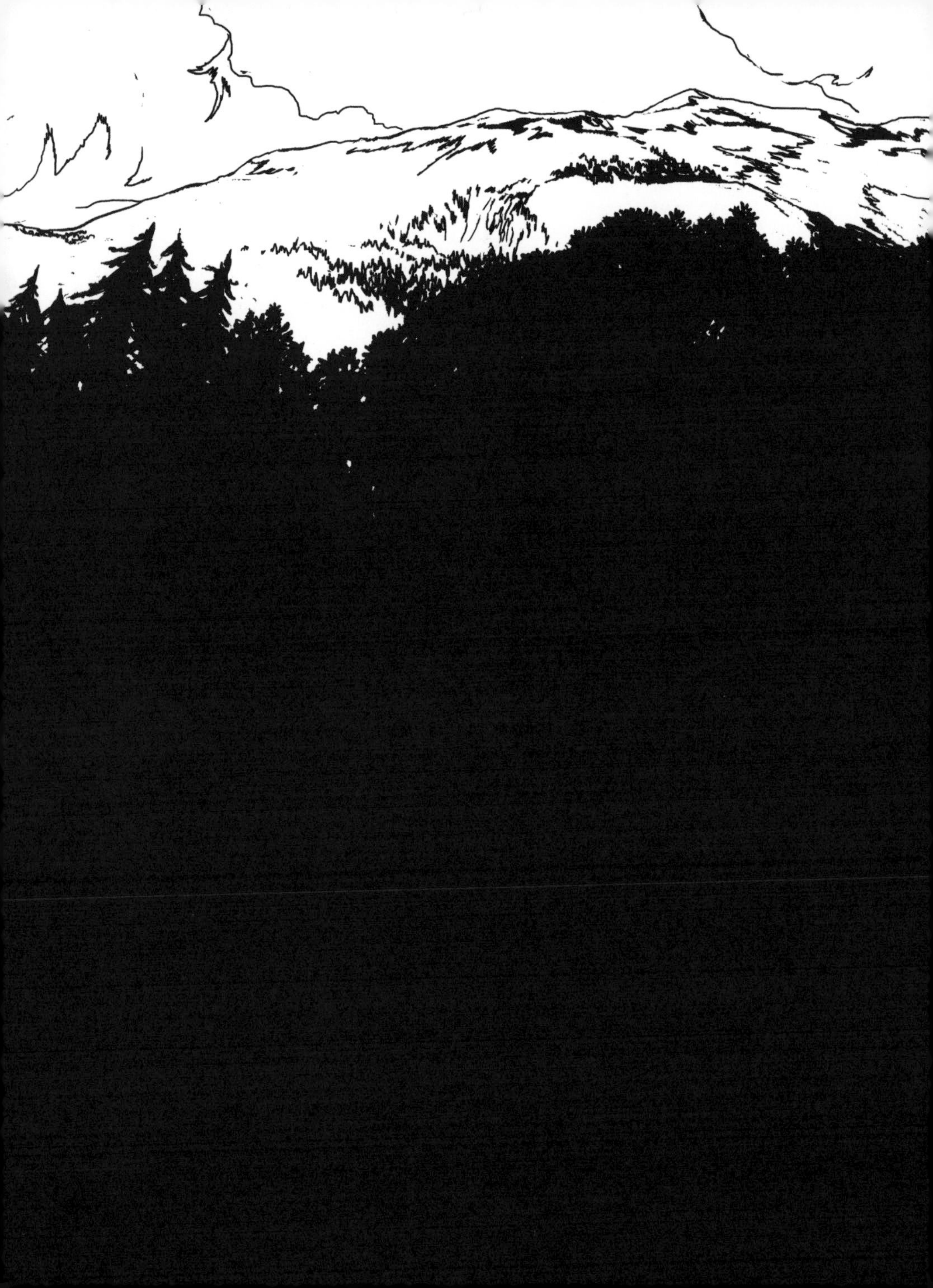

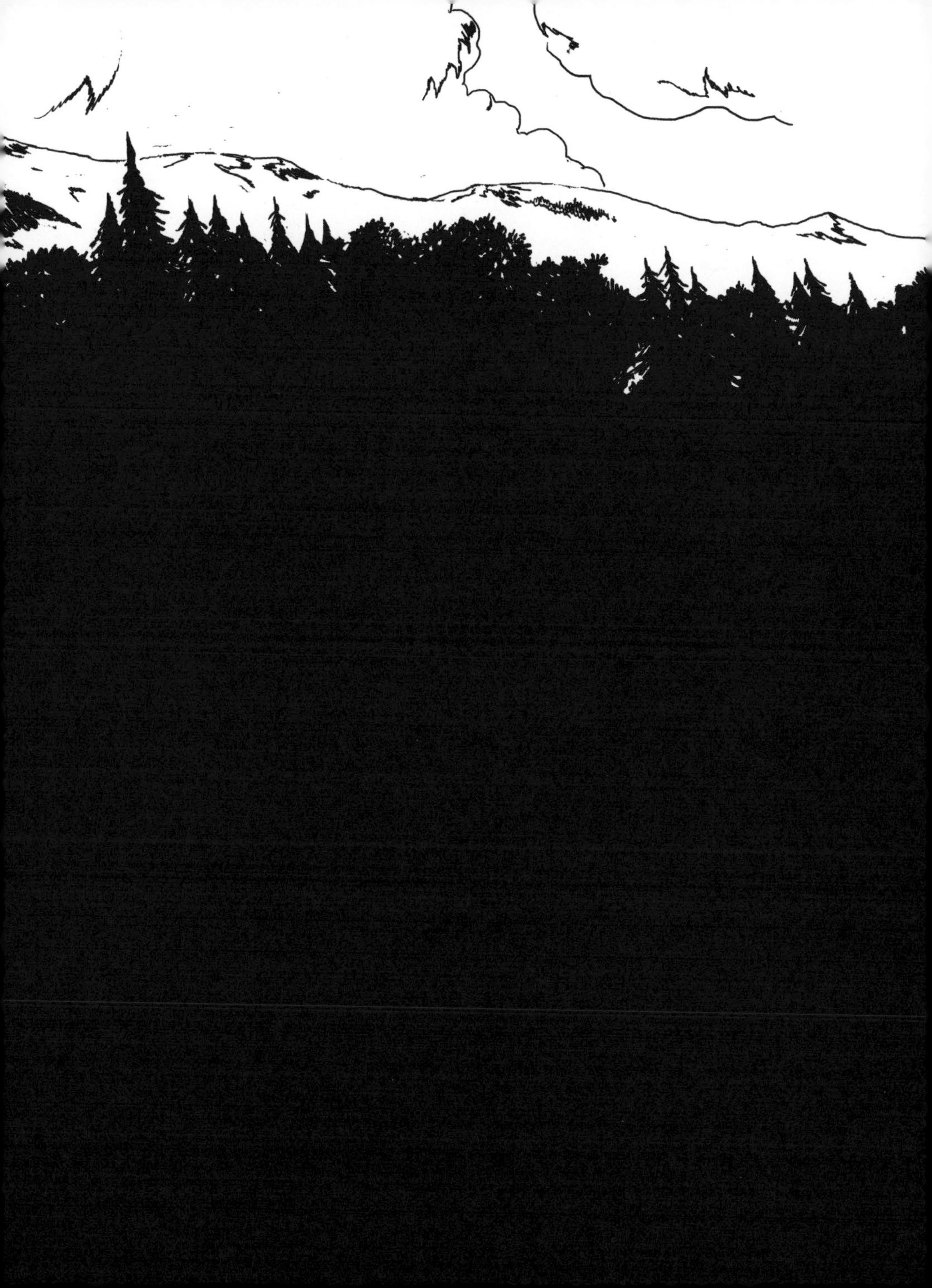

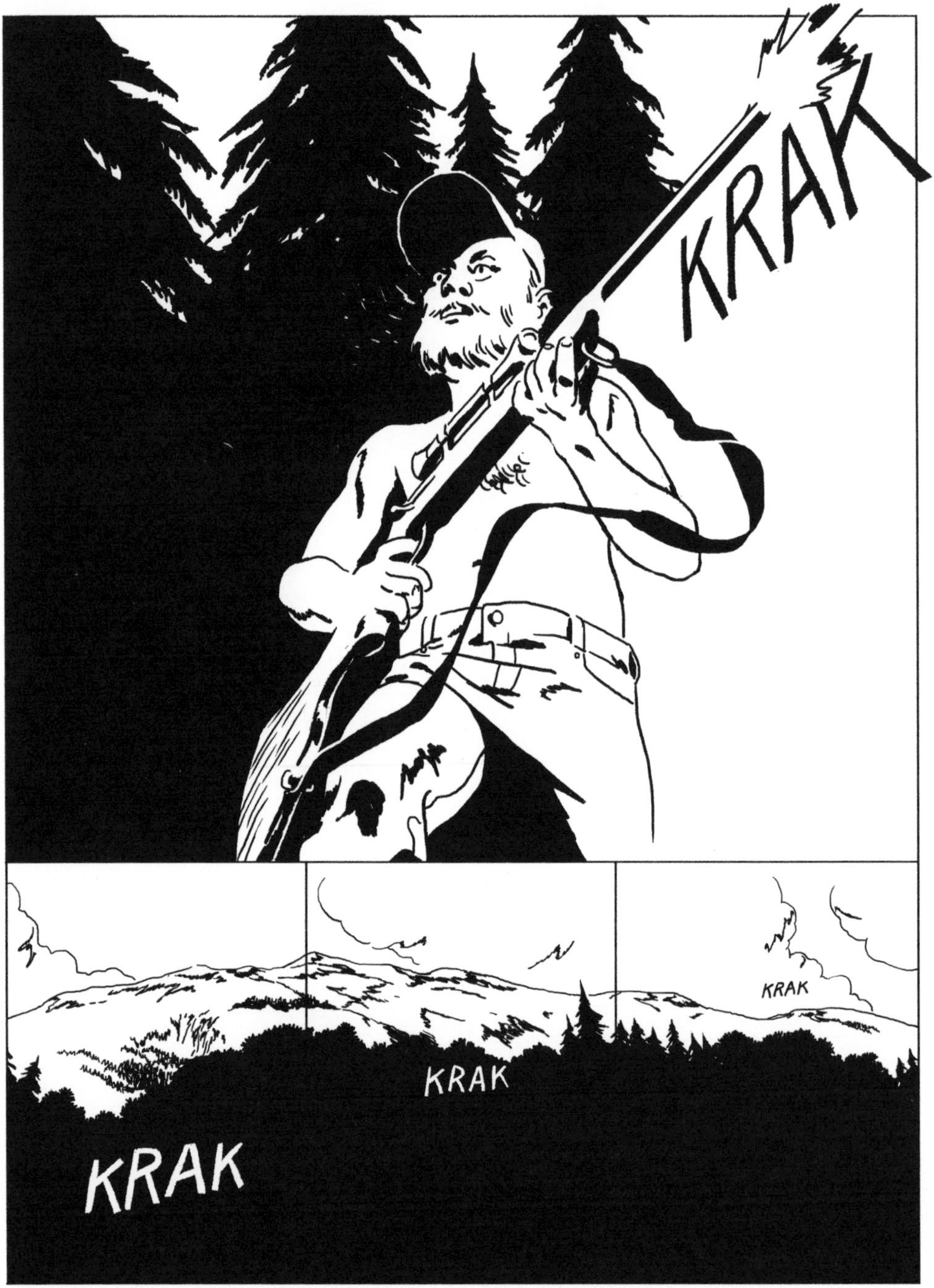
KRAK
KRAK
KRAK
KRAK

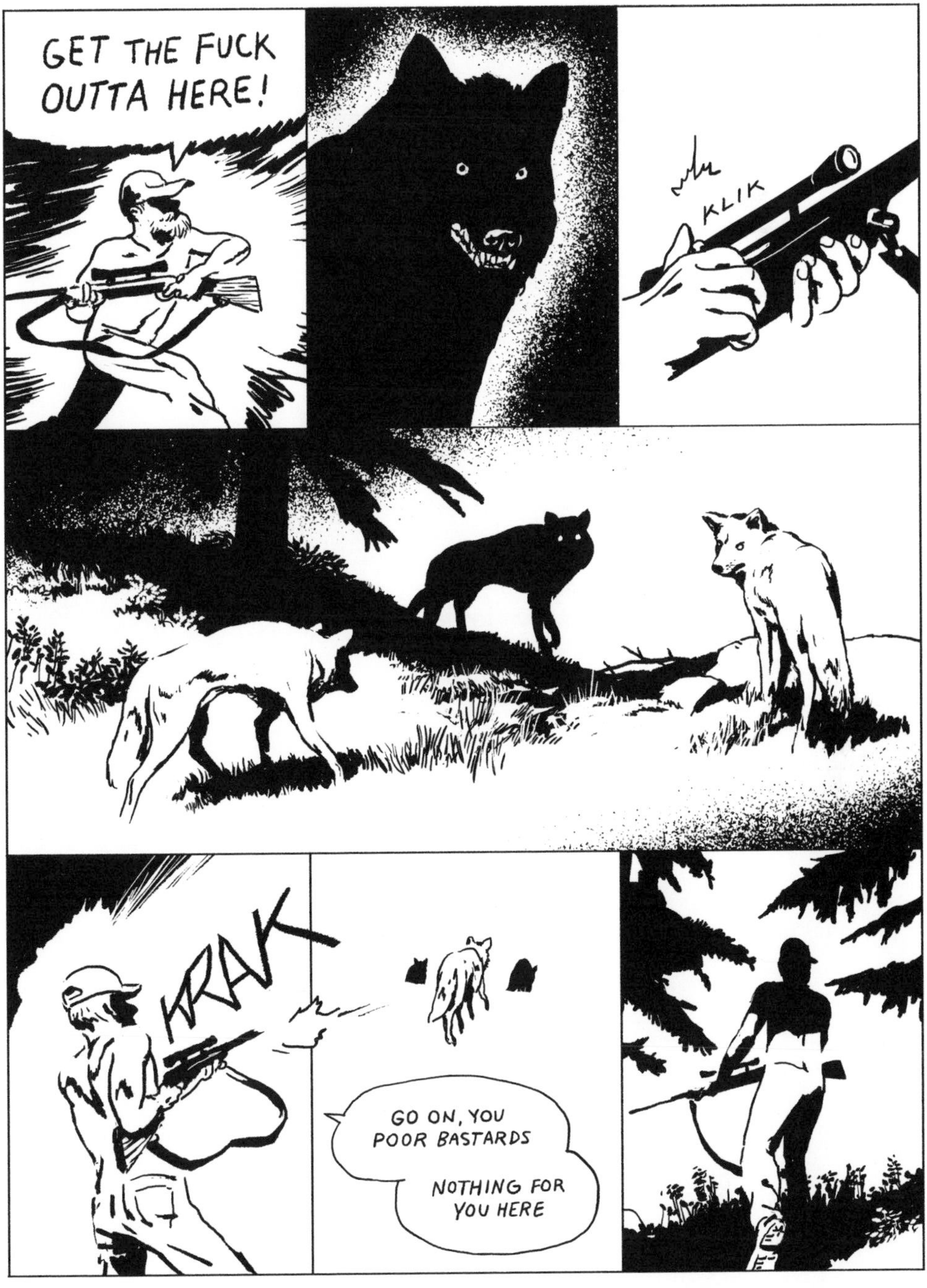
GET THE FUCK OUTTA HERE!
KLIK
KRAK
GO ON, YOU POOR BASTARDS
NOTHING FOR YOU HERE

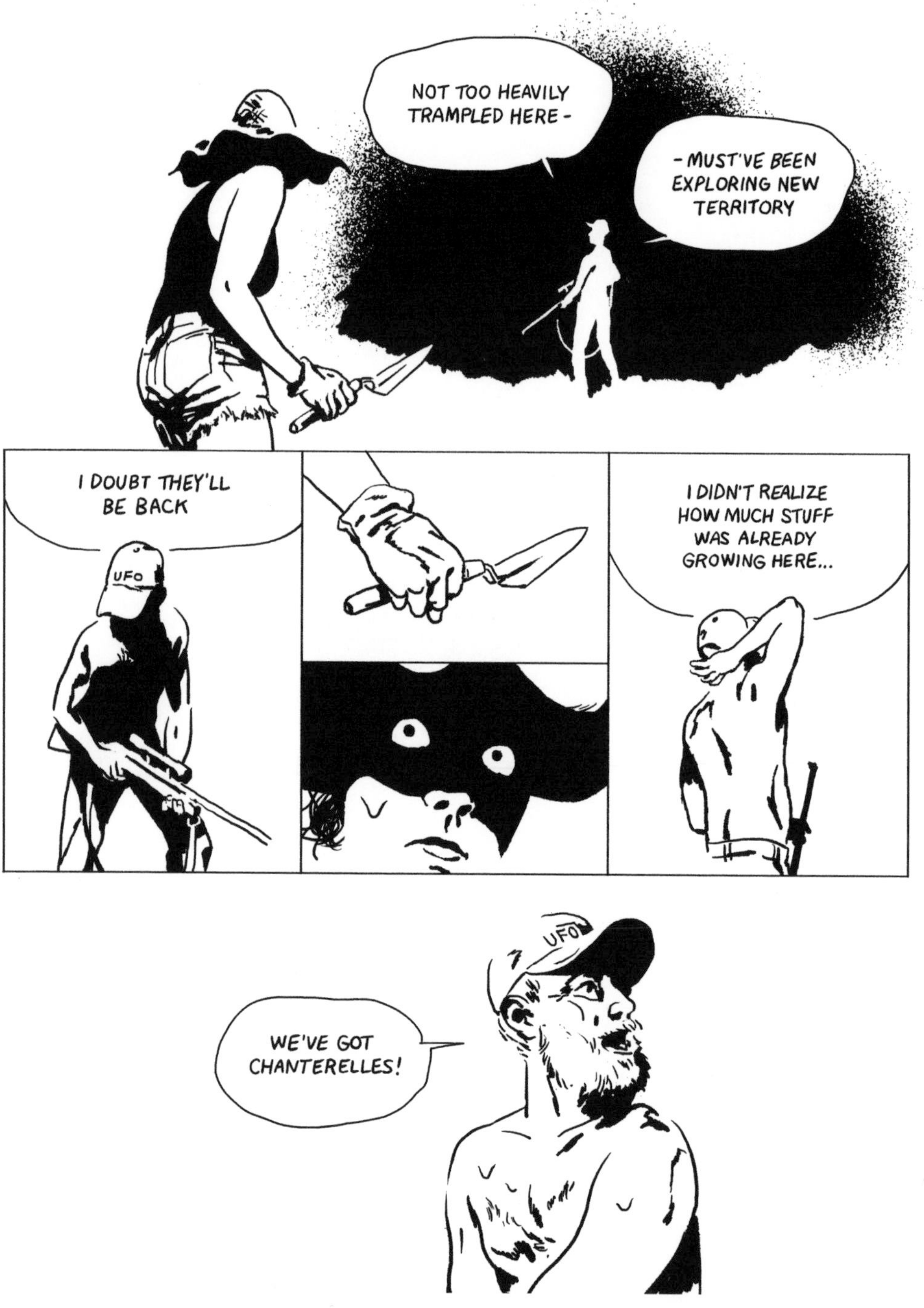
NOT TOO HEAVILY TRAMPLED HERE -
- MUST'VE BEEN EXPLORING NEW TERRITORY
I DOUBT THEY'LL BE BACK
UFO
I DIDN'T REALIZE HOW MUCH STUFF WAS ALREADY GROWING HERE...
UFO
WE'VE GOT CHANTERELLES!

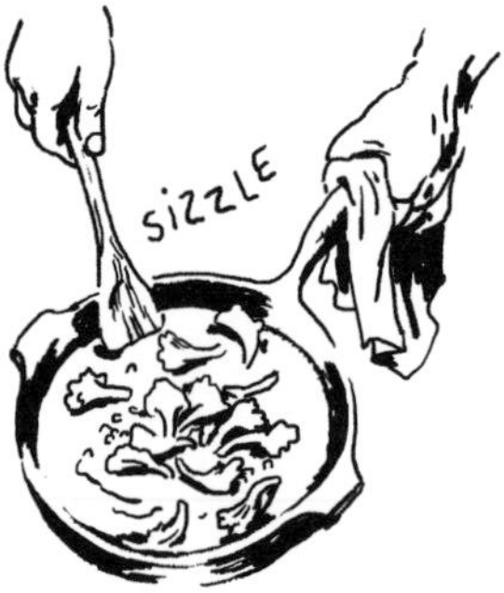
SIZZLE

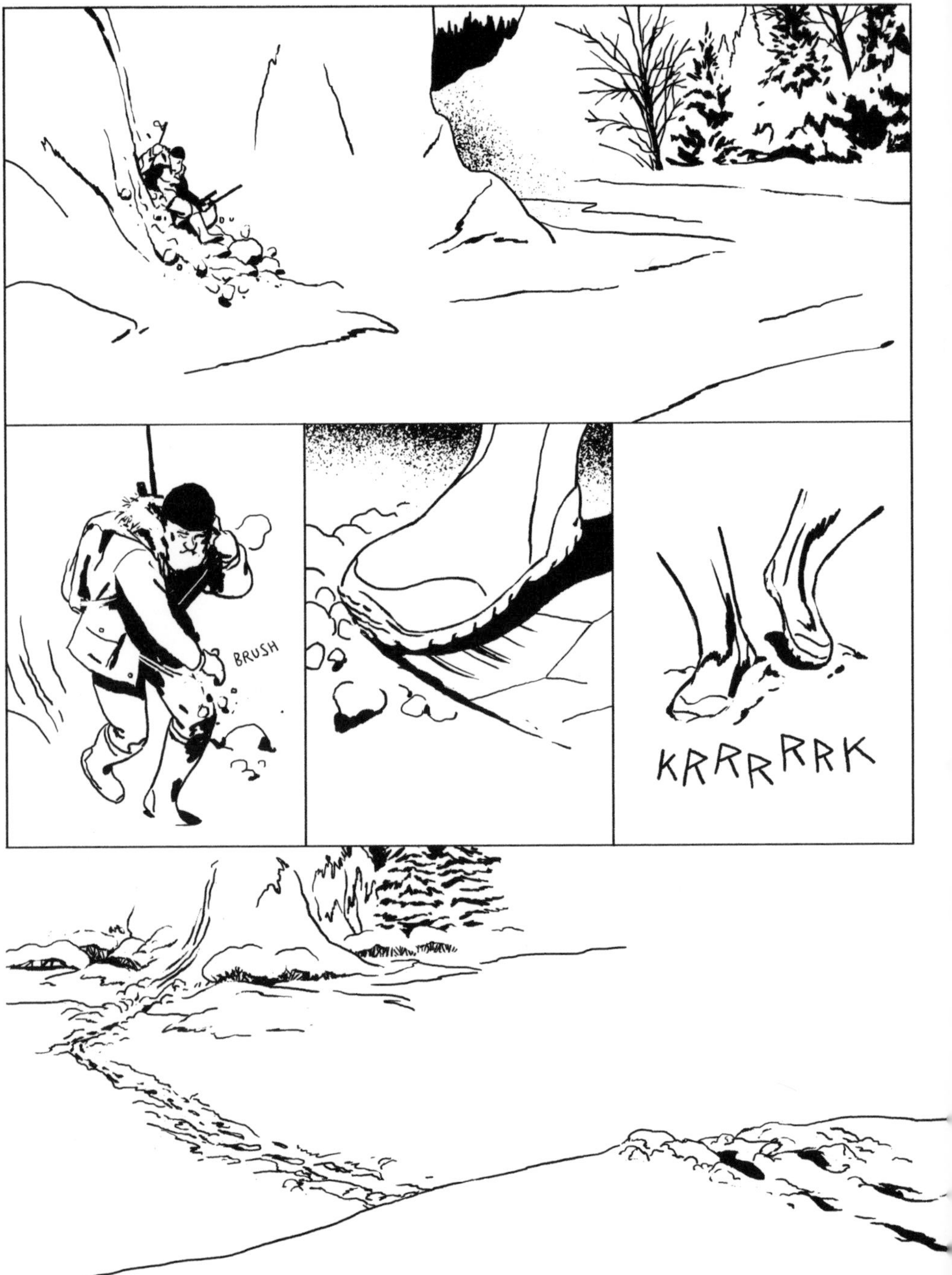
BRUSH
KRRRRRK

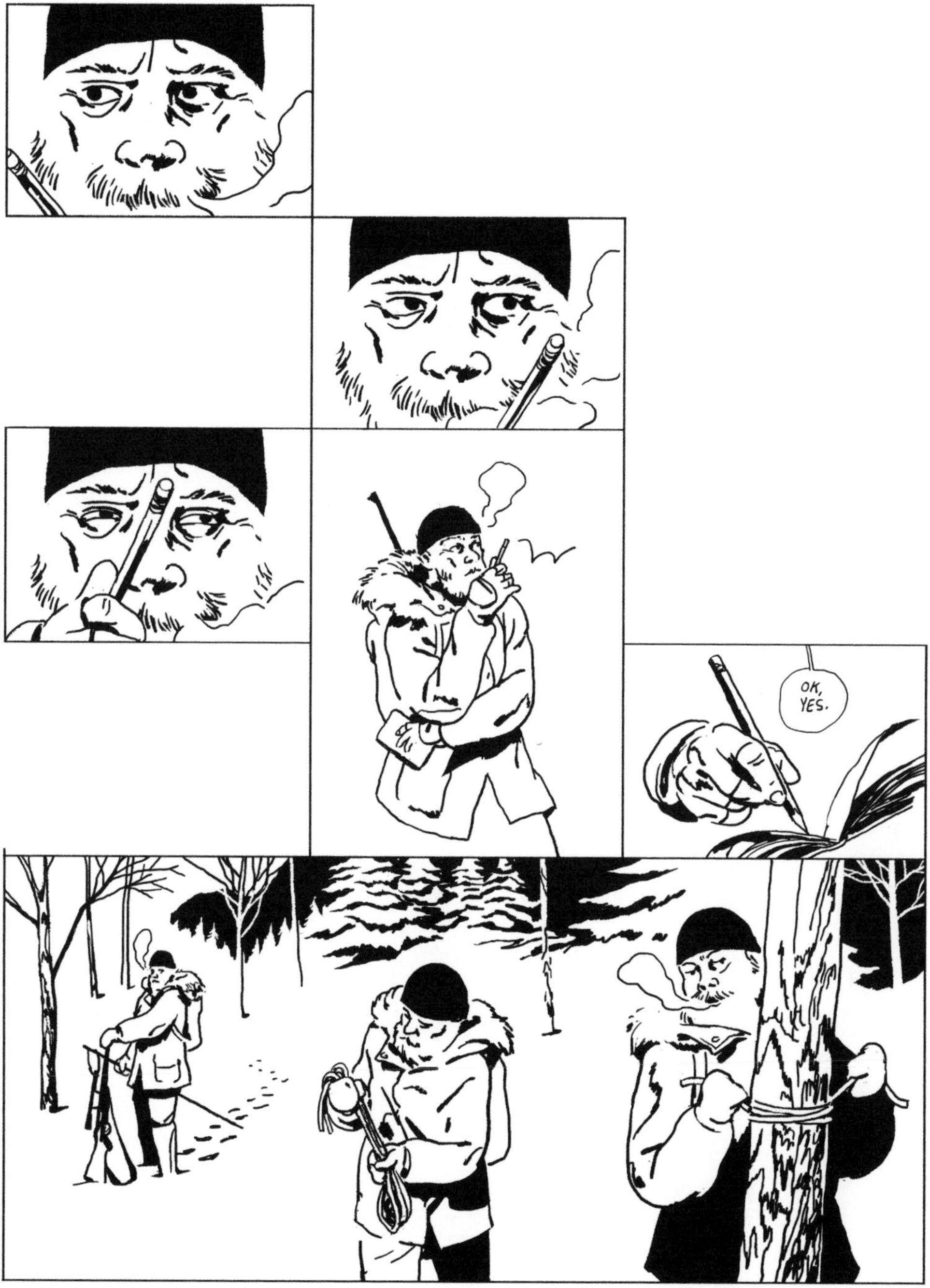
OK,
YES.

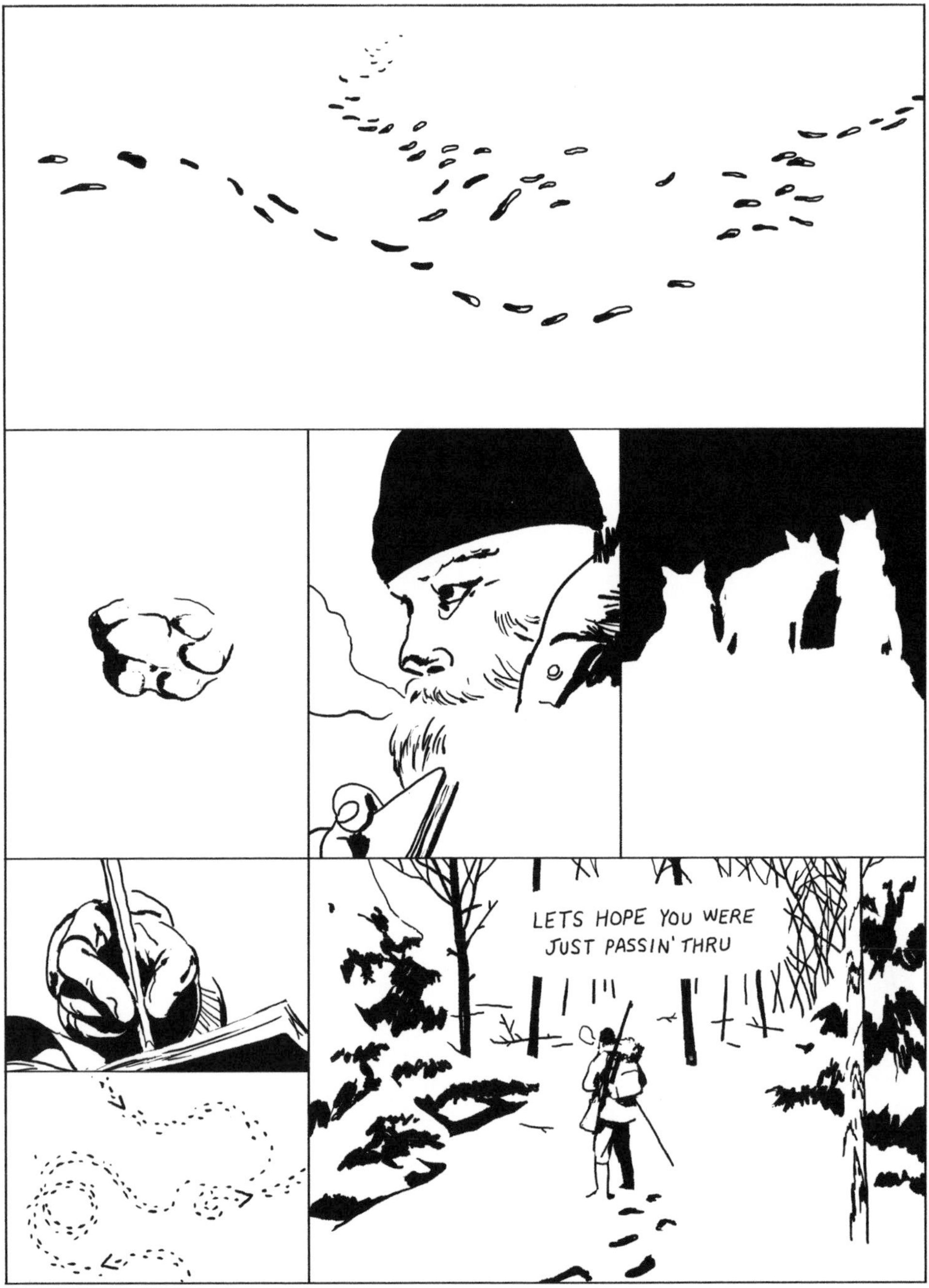
LETS HOPE YOU WERE
JUST PASSIN' THRU

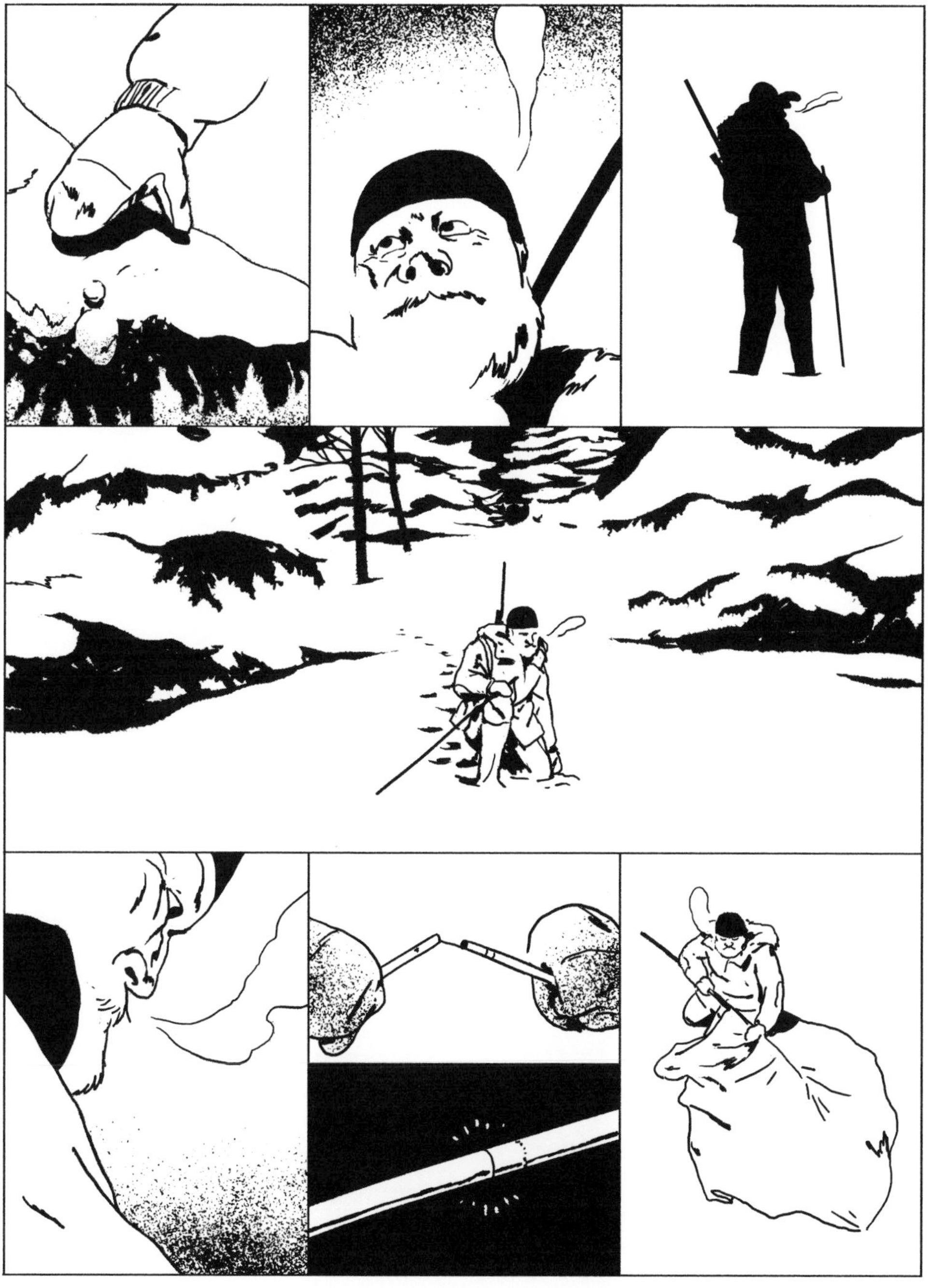

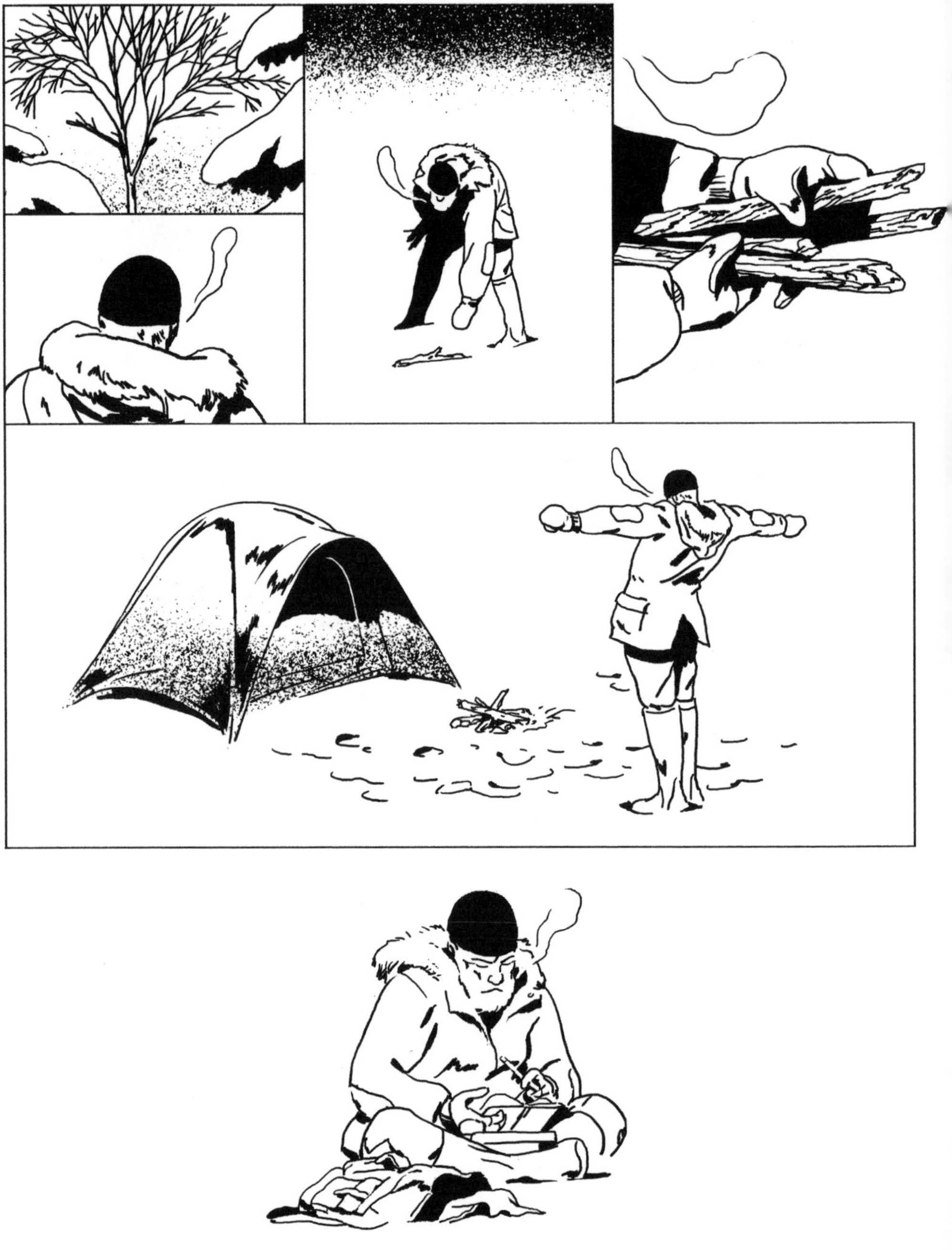

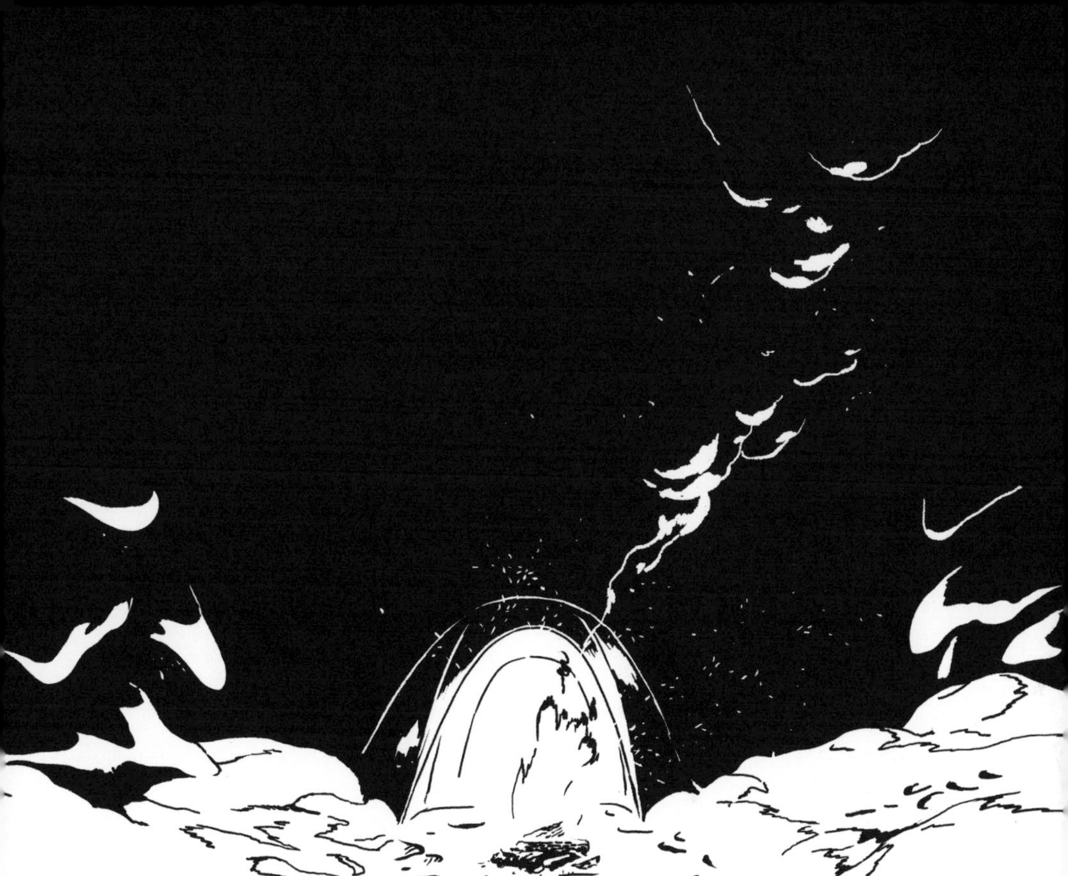

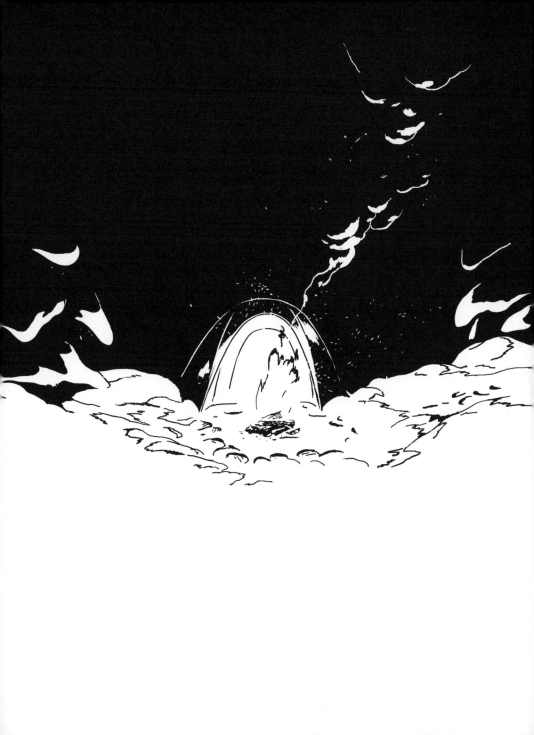

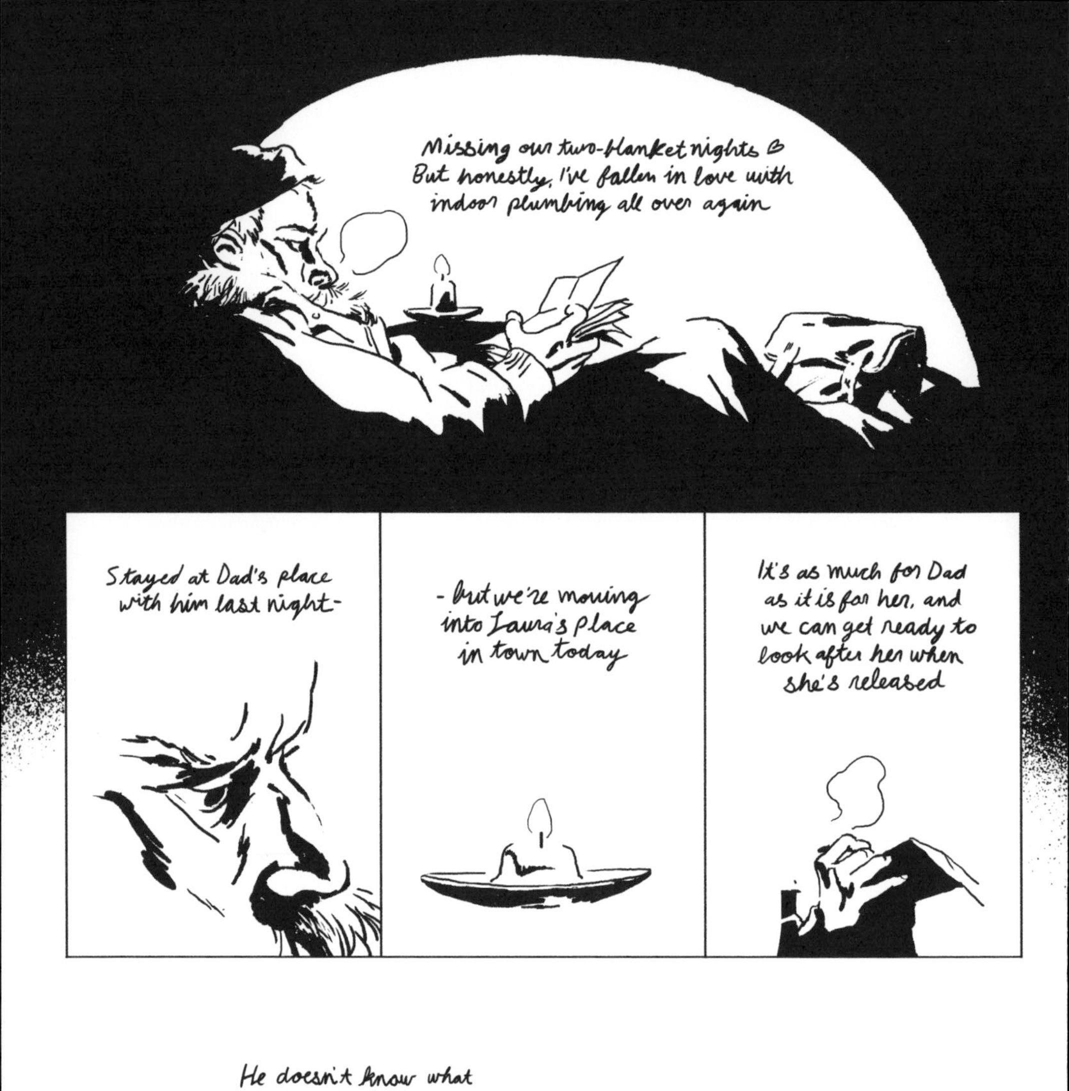
Missing our two-blanket nights ♡ But honestly, I've fallen in love with indoor plumbing all over again
Stayed at Dad's place with him last night-
- but we're moving into Laura's place in town today
It's as much for Dad as it is for her, and we can get ready to look after her when she's released
He doesn't know what to do with himself...
I think I can keep him distracted

writing that out just
now makes me realize – – this whole thing
is keeping me
distracted too

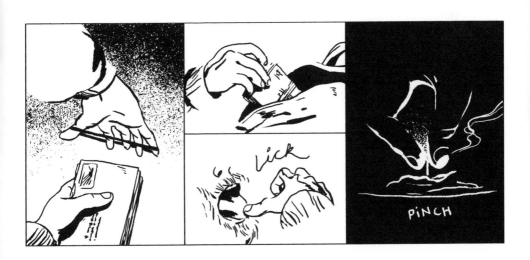

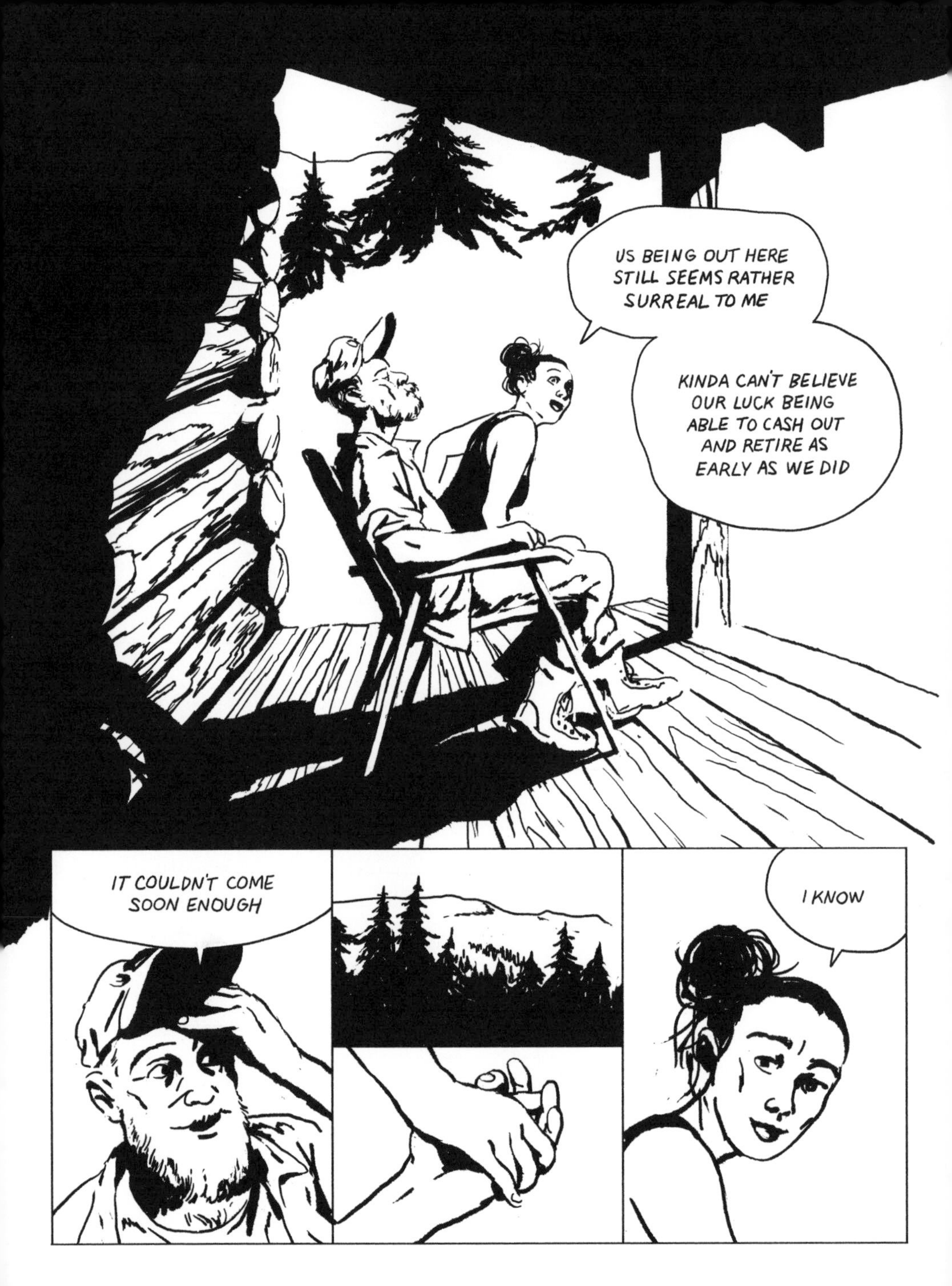
US BEING OUT HERE STILL SEEMS RATHER SURREAL TO ME
KINDA CAN'T BELIEVE OUR LUCK BEING ABLE TO CASH OUT AND RETIRE AS EARLY AS WE DID
IT COULDN'T COME SOON ENOUGH
I KNOW

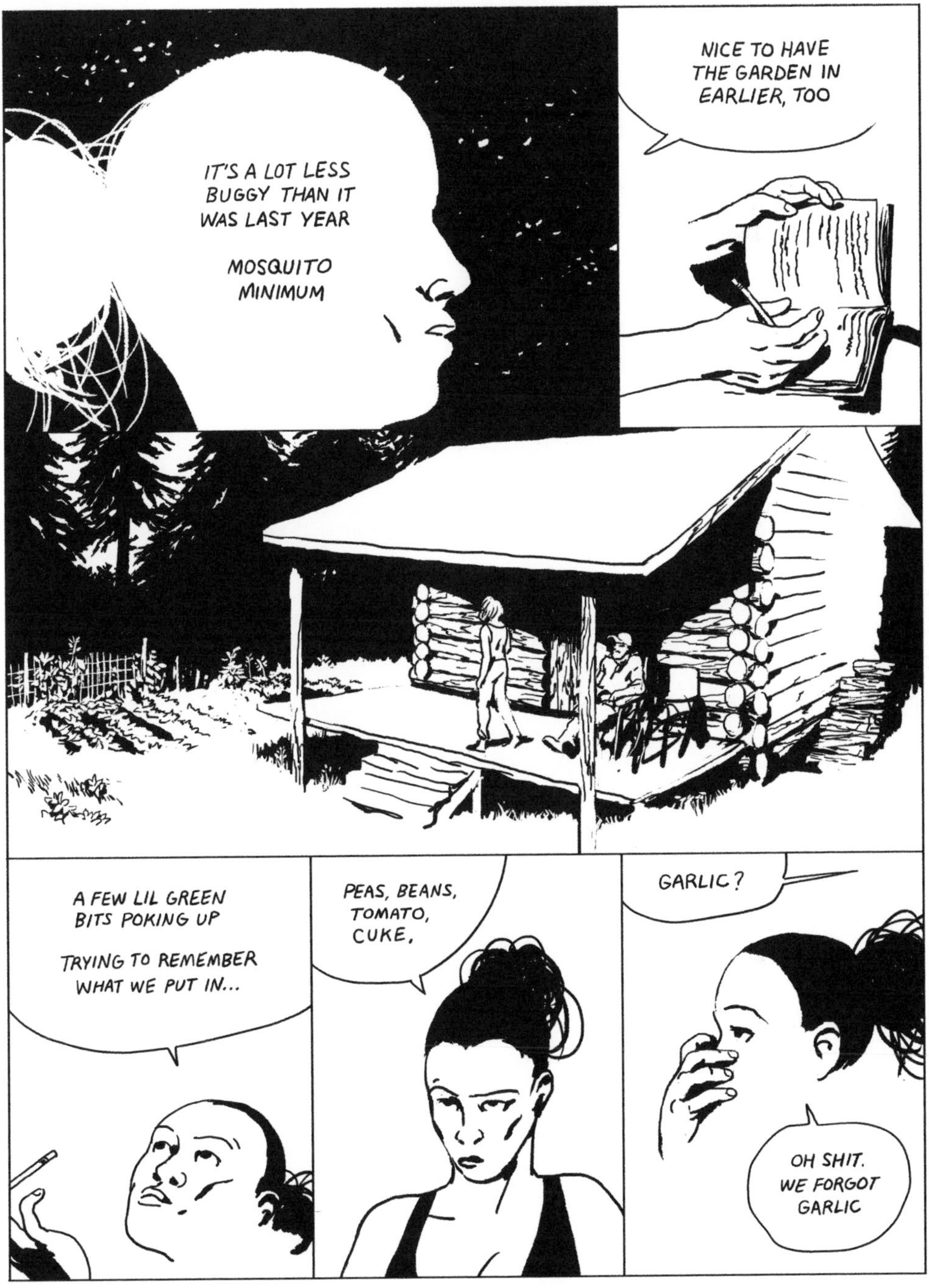
IT'S A LOT LESS BUGGY THAN IT WAS LAST YEAR
MOSQUITO MINIMUM
NICE TO HAVE THE GARDEN IN EARLIER, TOO
A FEW LIL GREEN BITS POKING UP
TRYING TO REMEMBER WHAT WE PUT IN...
PEAS, BEANS, TOMATO, CUKE,
GARLIC?
OH SHIT. WE FORGOT GARLIC

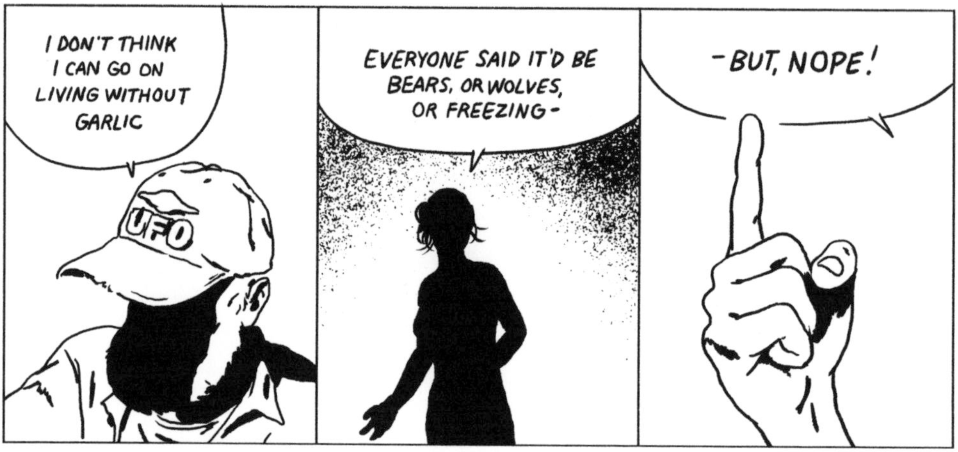
I DON'T THINK I CAN GO ON LIVING WITHOUT GARLIC
UFO
EVERYONE SAID IT'D BE BEARS, OR WOLVES, OR FREEZING-
-BUT, NOPE!

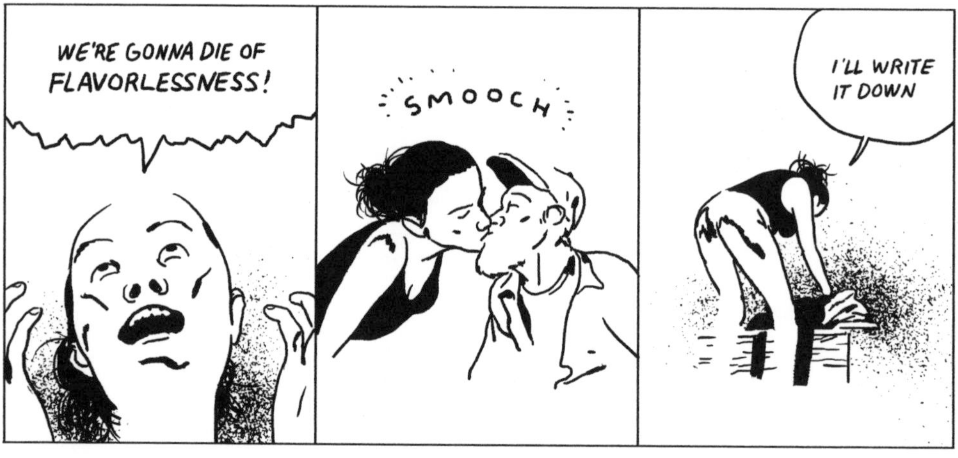
WE'RE GONNA DIE OF FLAVORLESSNESS!
SMOOCH
I'LL WRITE IT DOWN

WE NEED A FEW STAPLES ANYWAY
MATCHES,
TOOTHPASTE,
OLIVE OIL.
I NEED NEW BOOTS
Y'THINK?
NEED SOME ROPE, TOO
A NEW COMPASS,
SOME SHELLS
REALLY WANNA COVER SOME GROUND BEFORE THE SNOW FLIES

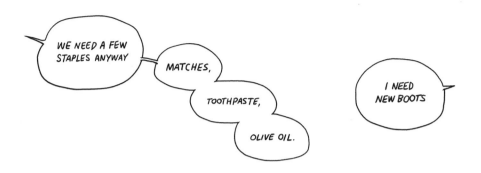

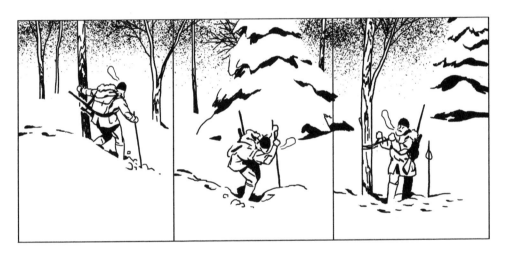

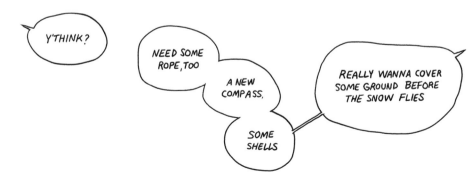

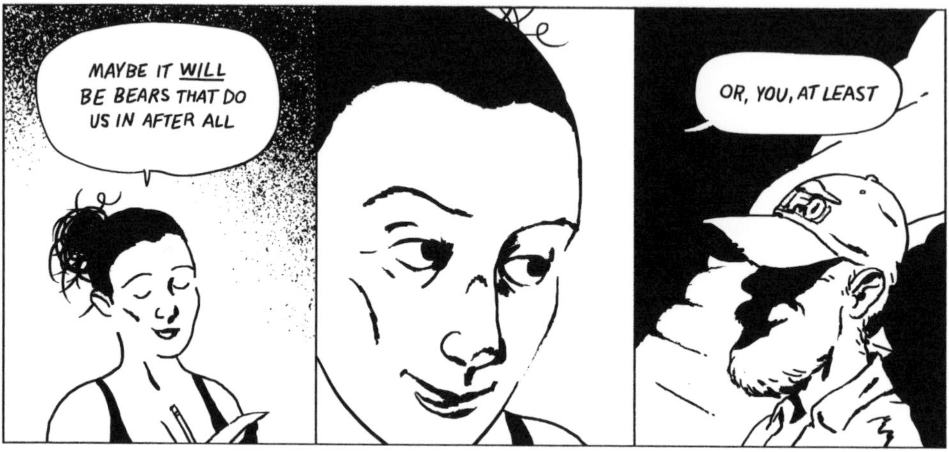
MAYBE IT WILL BE BEARS THAT DO US IN AFTER ALL
OR, YOU, AT LEAST
UFO

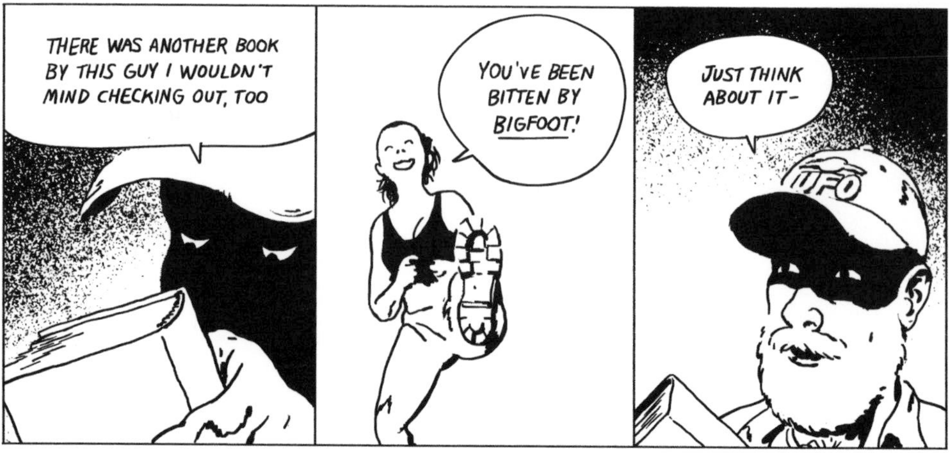
THERE WAS ANOTHER BOOK BY THIS GUY I WOULDN'T MIND CHECKING OUT, TOO
YOU'VE BEEN BITTEN BY BIGFOOT!
JUST THINK ABOUT IT-
UFO

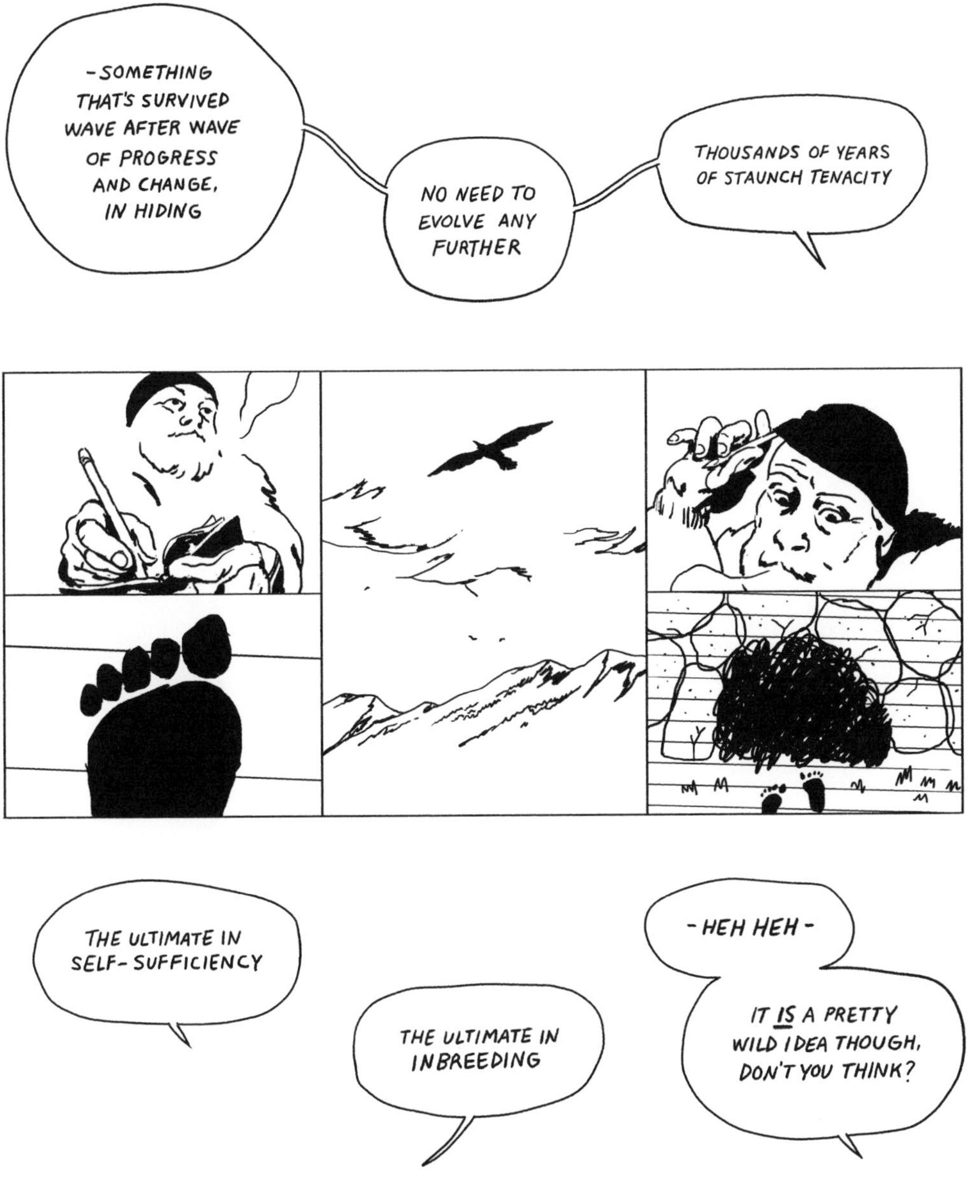
-SOMETHING THAT'S SURVIVED WAVE AFTER WAVE OF PROGRESS AND CHANGE, IN HIDING
NO NEED TO EVOLVE ANY FURTHER
THOUSANDS OF YEARS OF STAUNCH TENACITY
THE ULTIMATE IN SELF-SUFFICIENCY
THE ULTIMATE IN INBREEDING
-HEH HEH-
IT IS A PRETTY WILD IDEA THOUGH, DON'T YOU THINK?

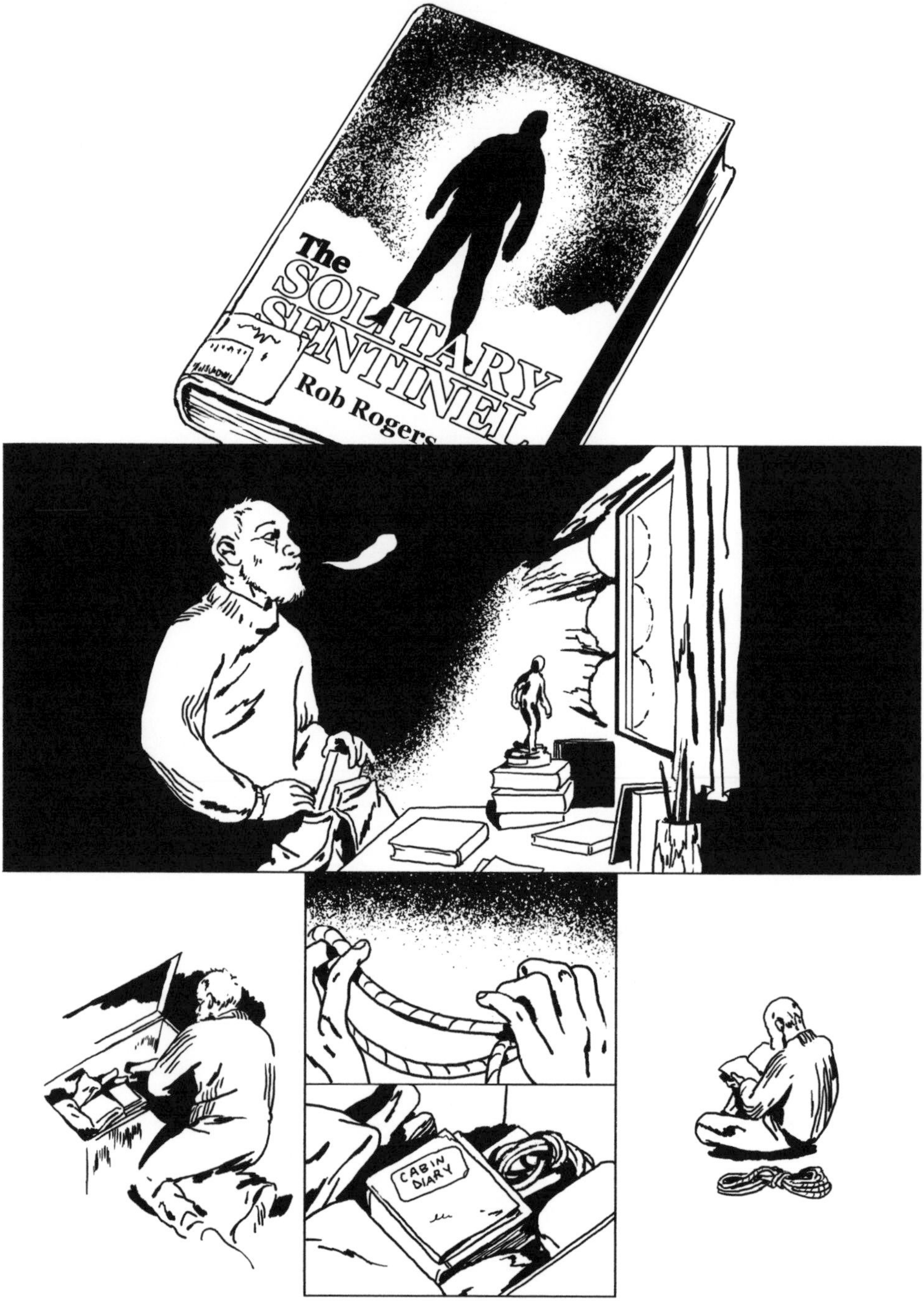
The
SOLITARY
SENTINEL
Rob Rogers
CABIN
DIARY

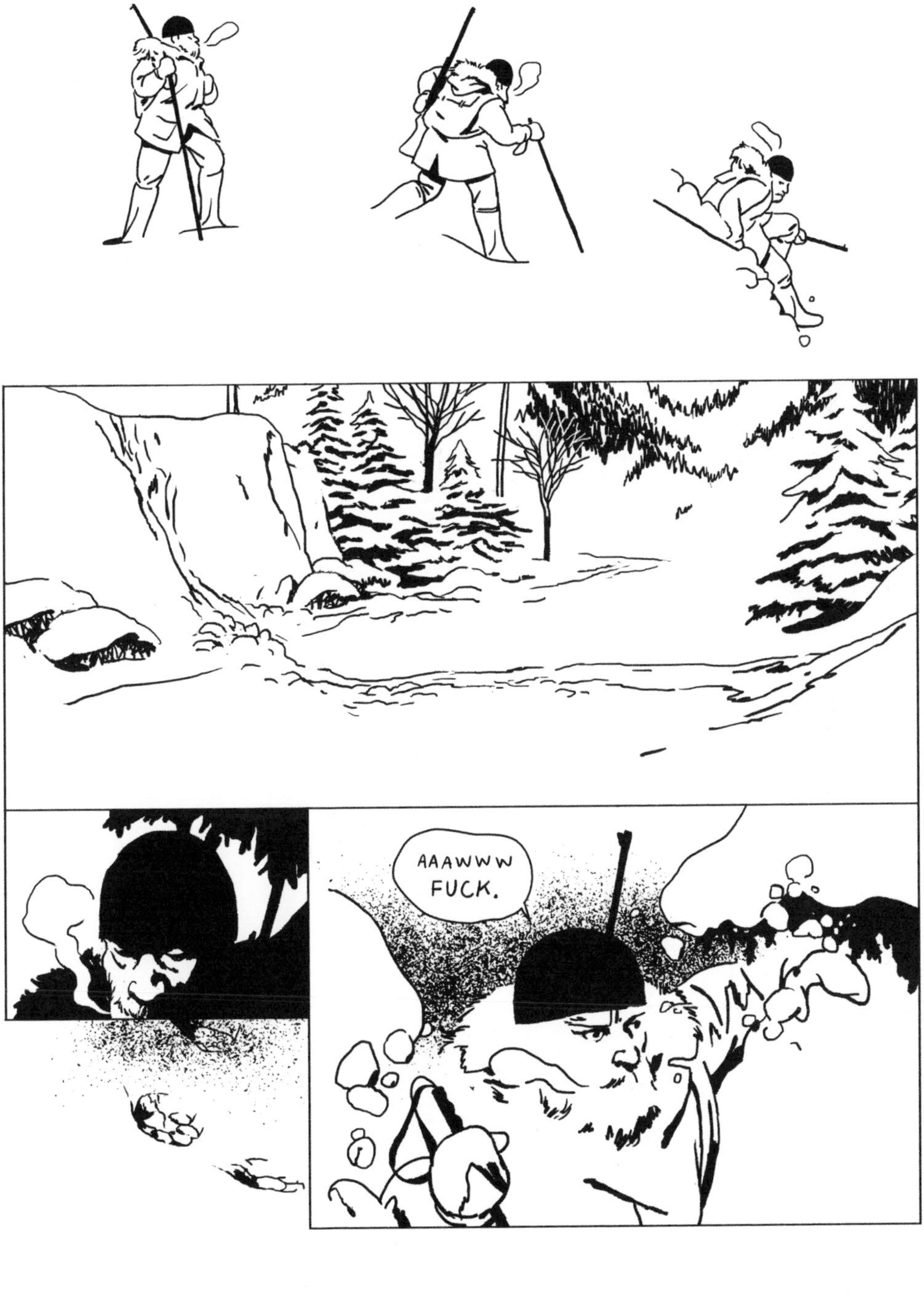
AAAWWW FUCK.

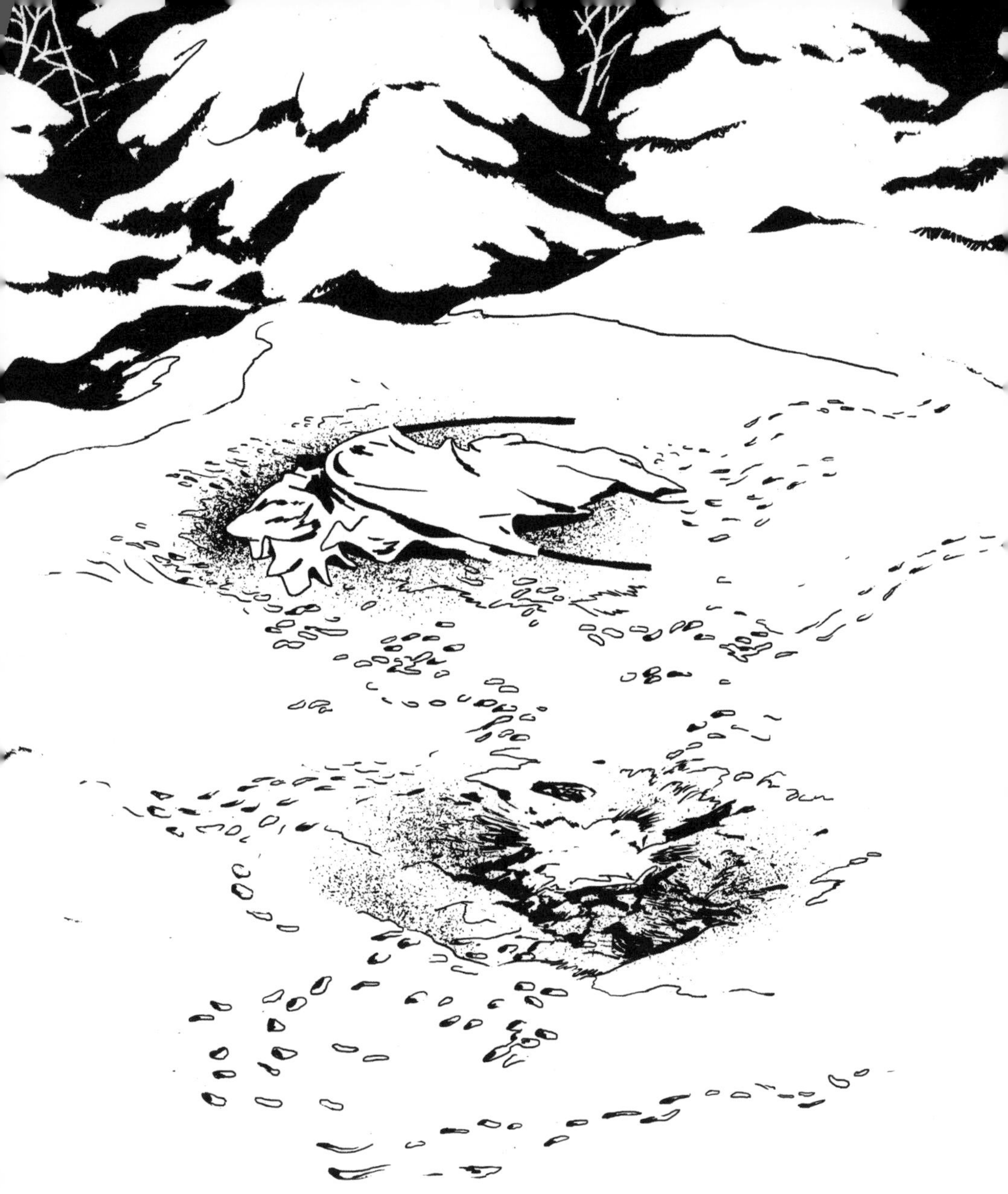

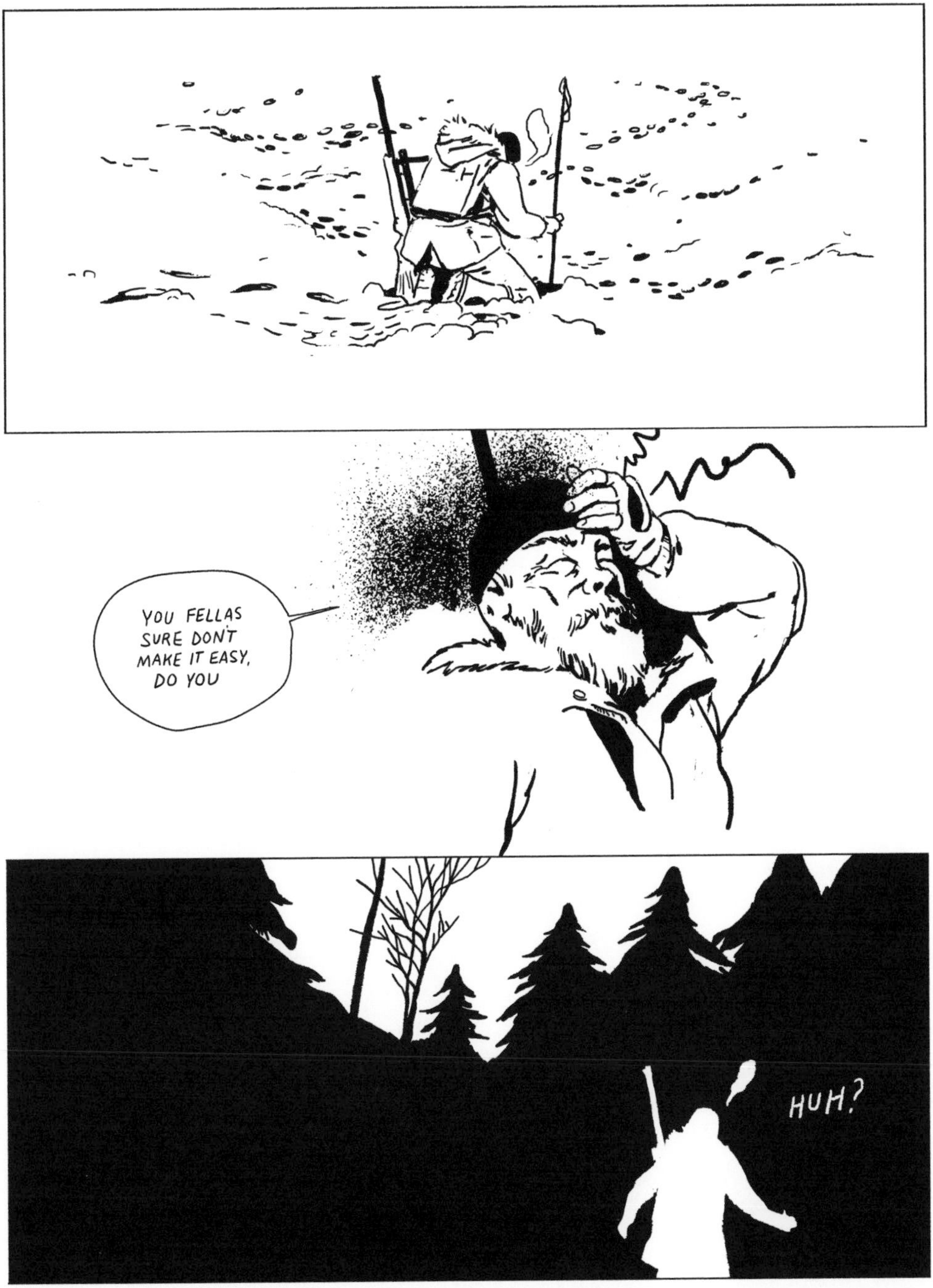
YOU FELLAS SURE DON'T MAKE IT EASY, DO YOU
HUH?

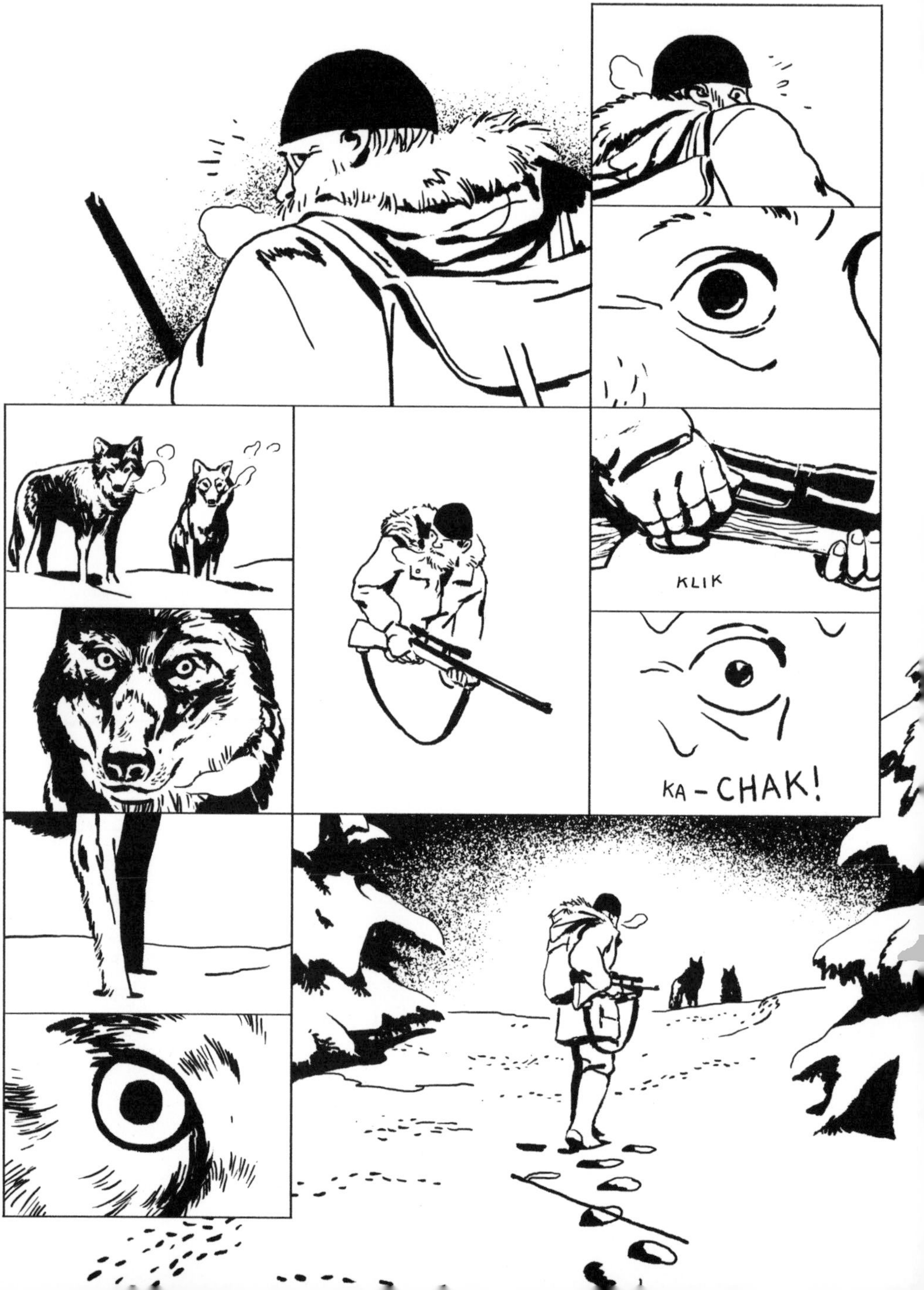
KLIK
KA-CHAK!

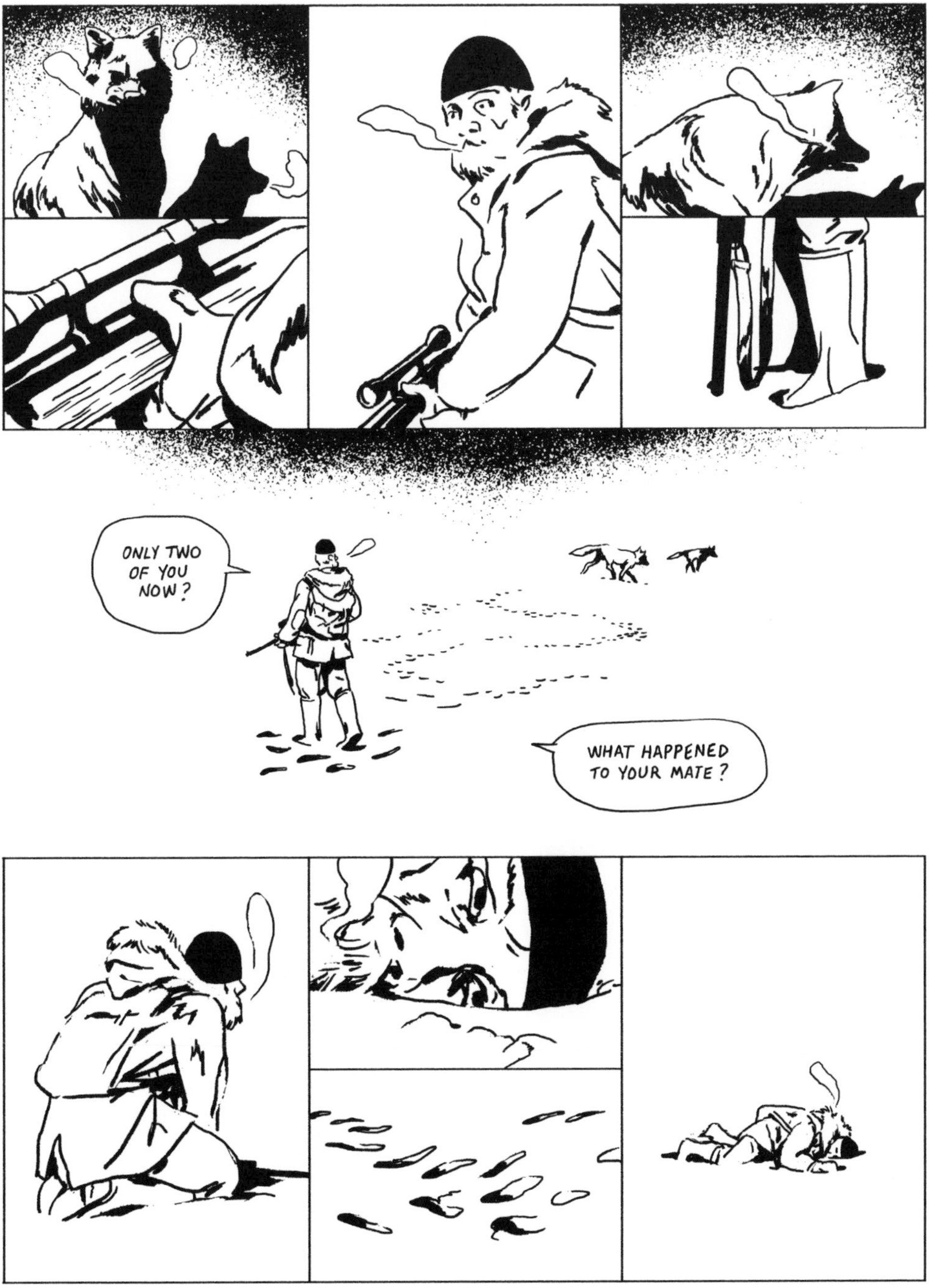
ONLY TWO OF YOU NOW?
WHAT HAPPENED TO YOUR MATE?

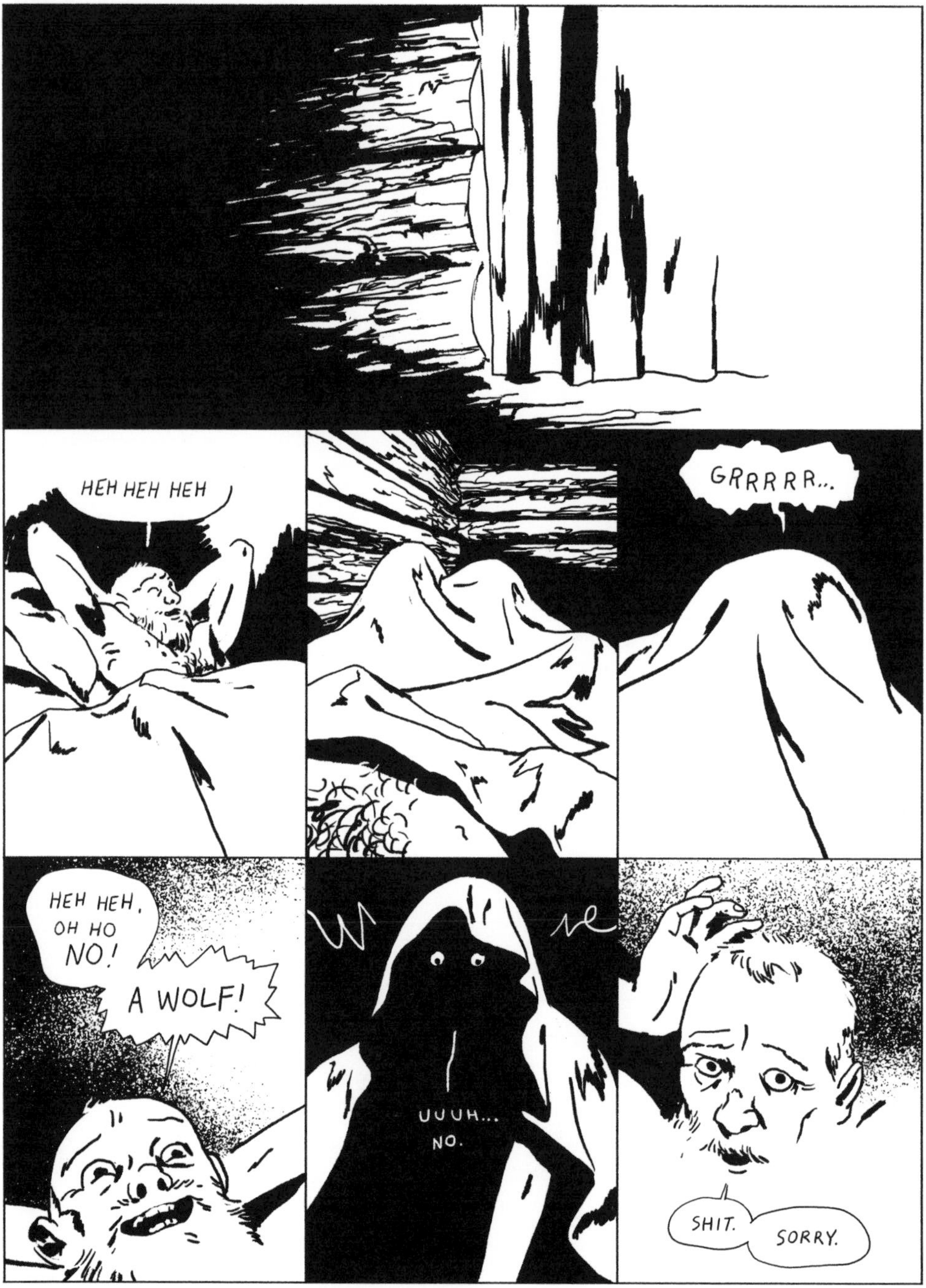
HEH HEH HEH
GRRRRR...
HEH HEH,
OH HO
NO!
A WOLF!
UUUH...
NO.
SHIT.
SORRY.

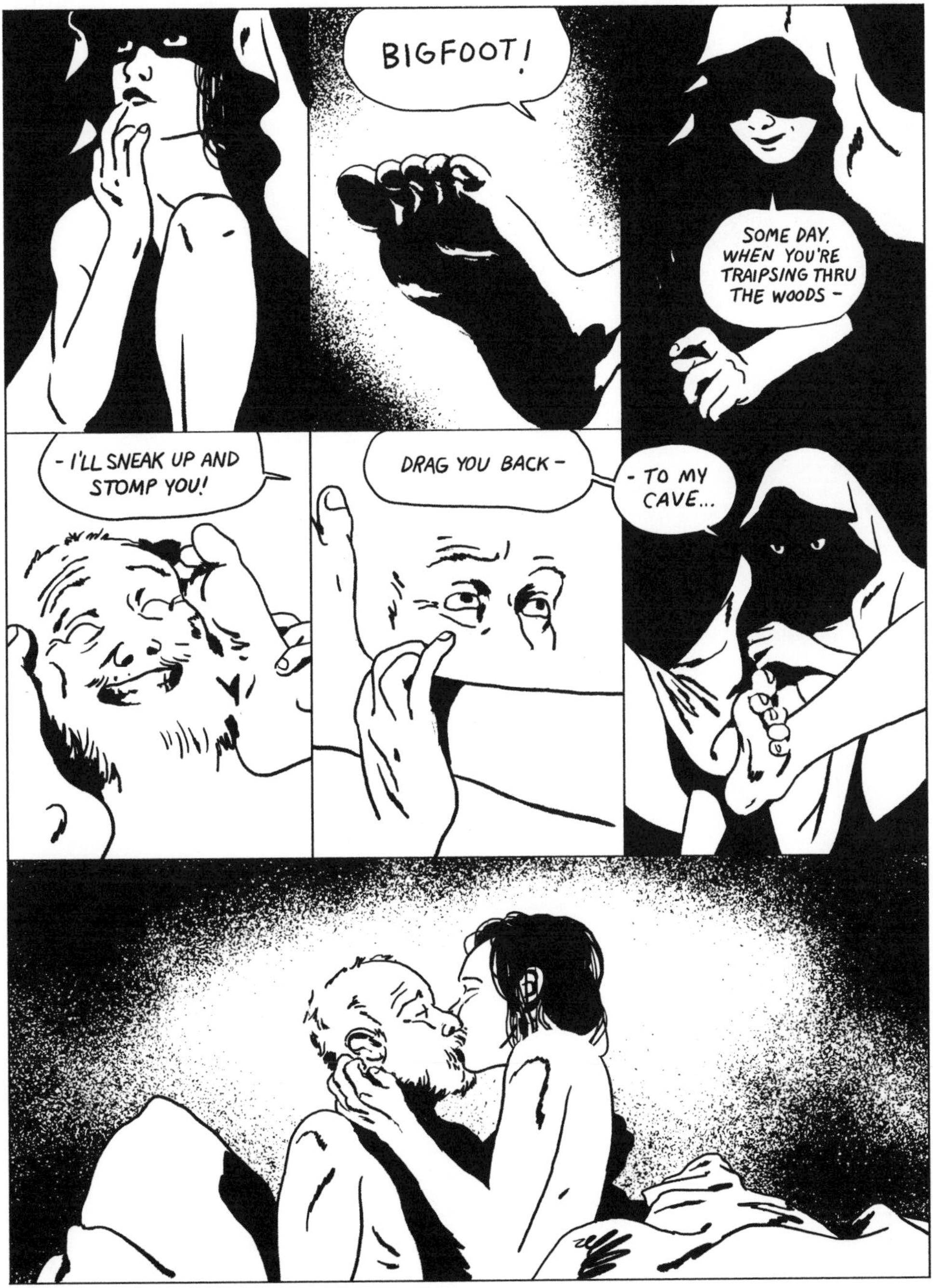
BIGFOOT!
SOME DAY, WHEN YOU'RE TRAIPSING THRU THE WOODS -
- I'LL SNEAK UP AND STOMP YOU!
DRAG YOU BACK -
- TO MY CAVE...

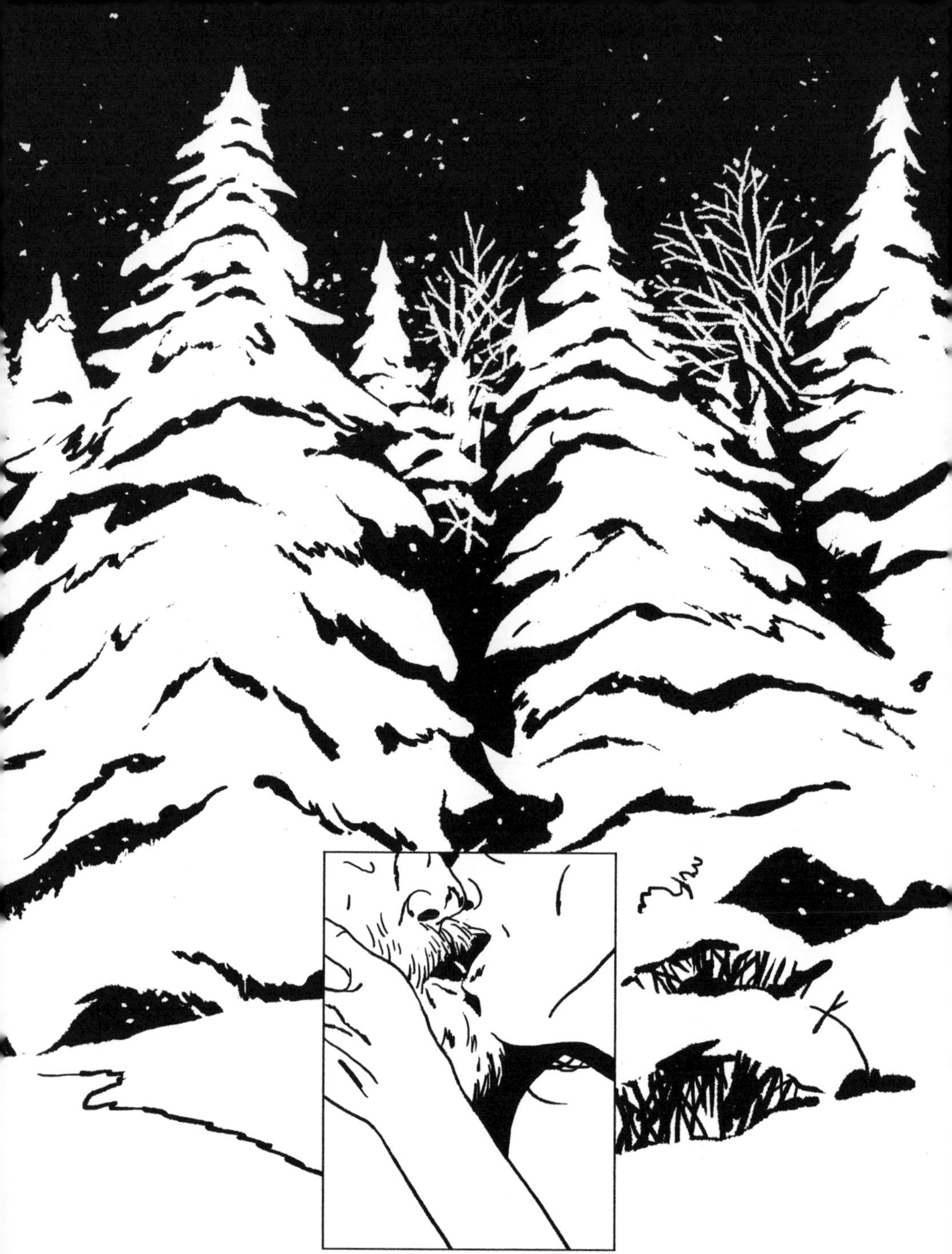

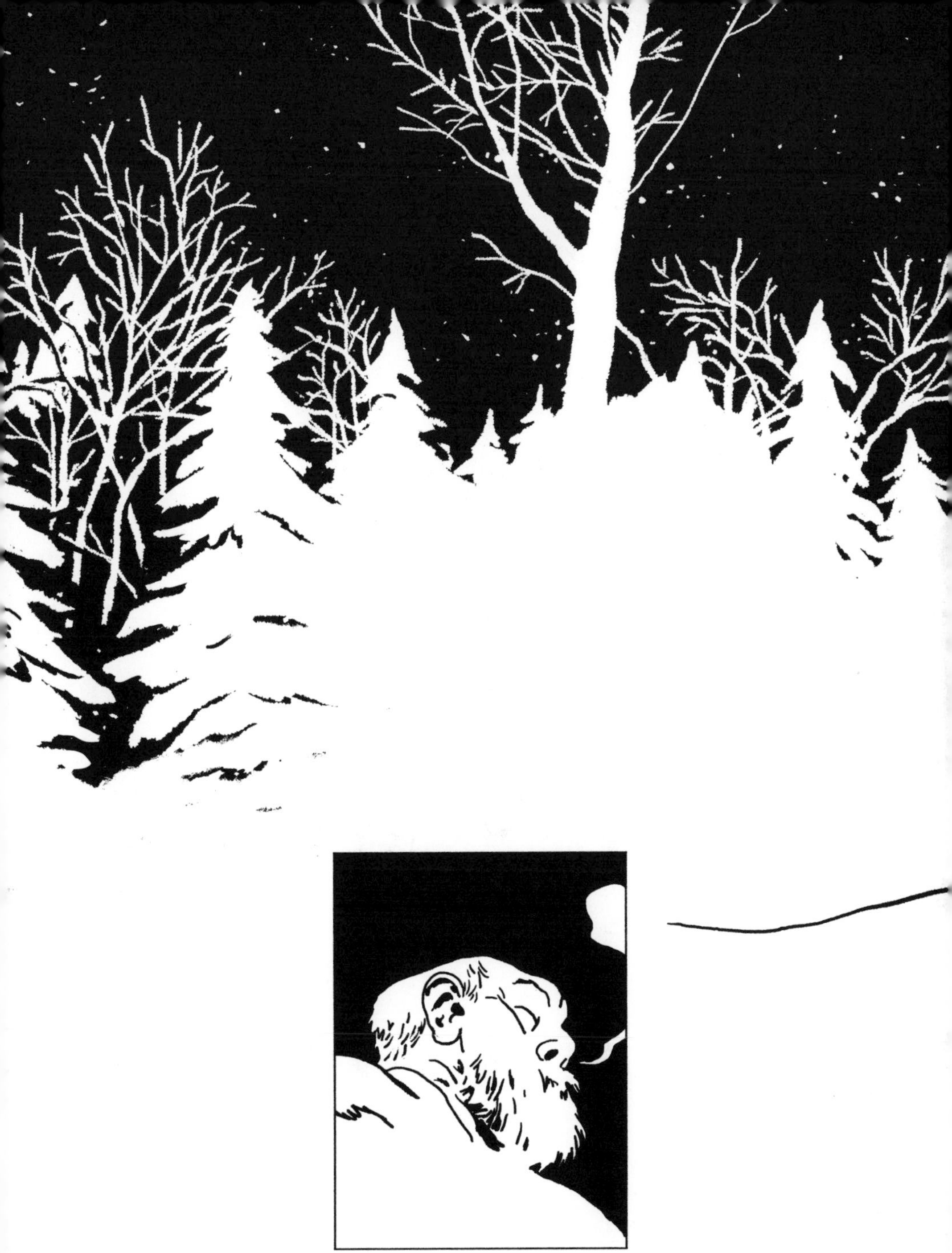

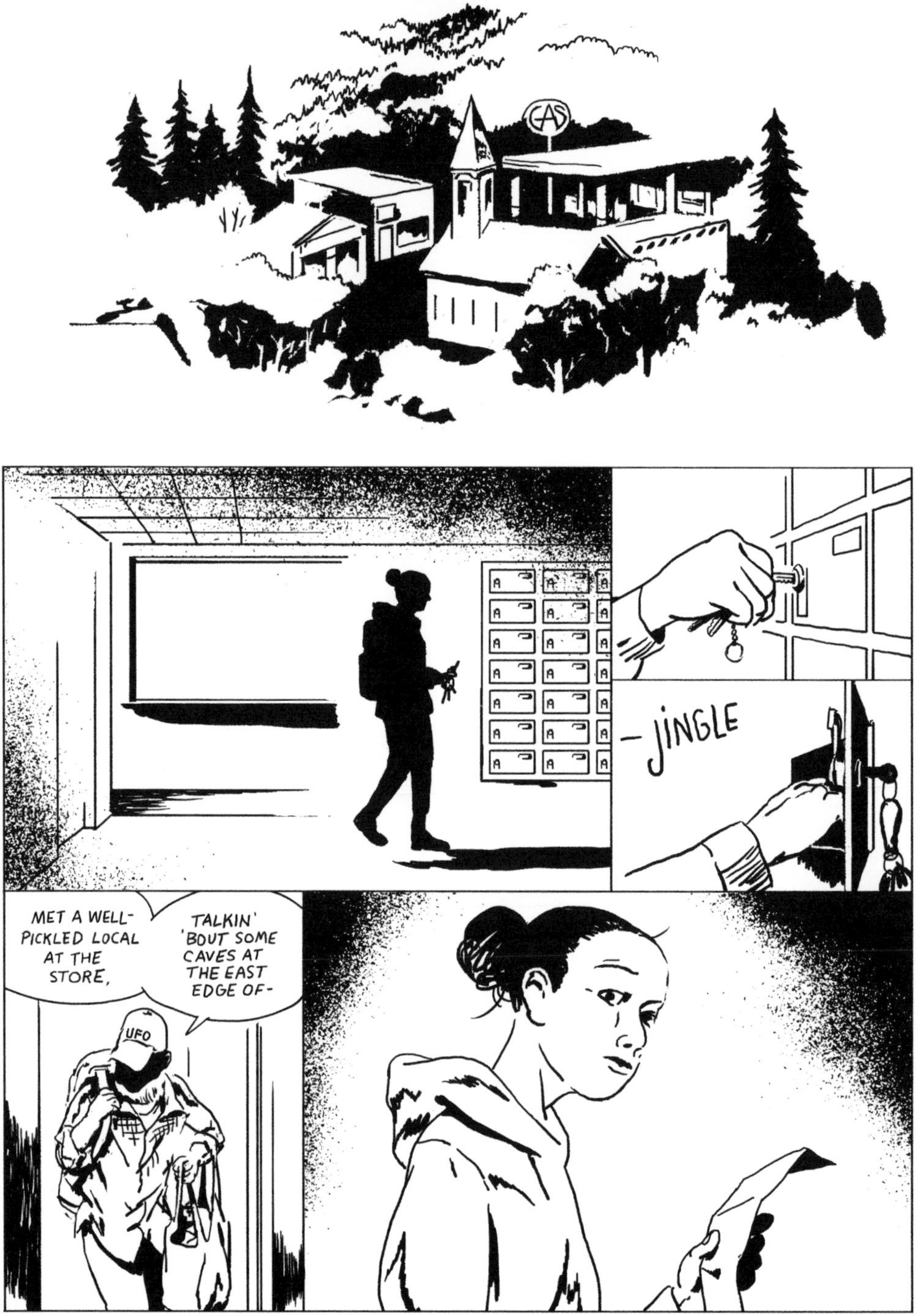
GAS
-JINGLE
MET A WELL-PICKLED LOCAL AT THE STORE,
TALKIN' 'BOUT SOME CAVES AT THE EAST EDGE OF-
UFO

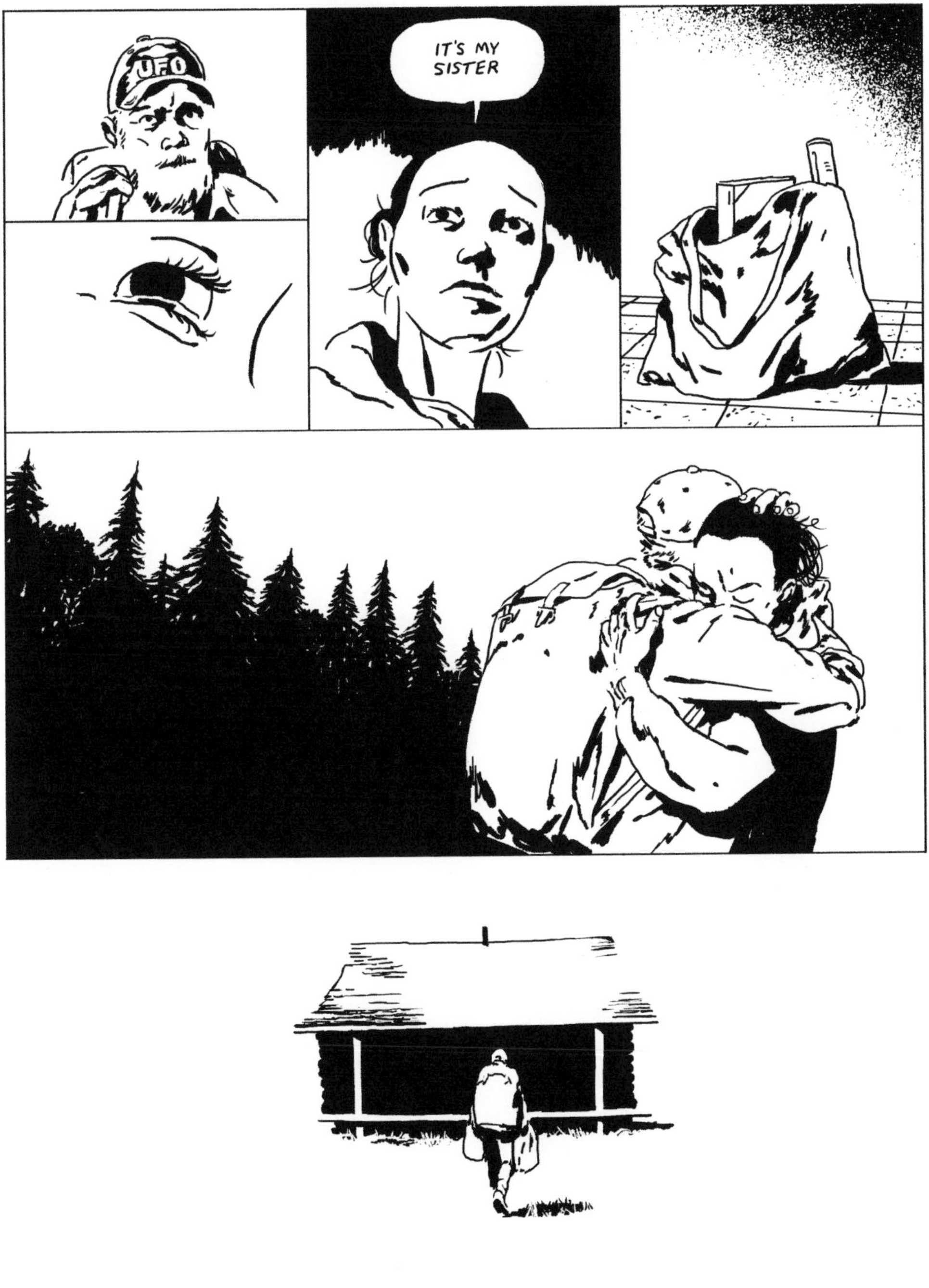
UFO
IT'S MY SISTER

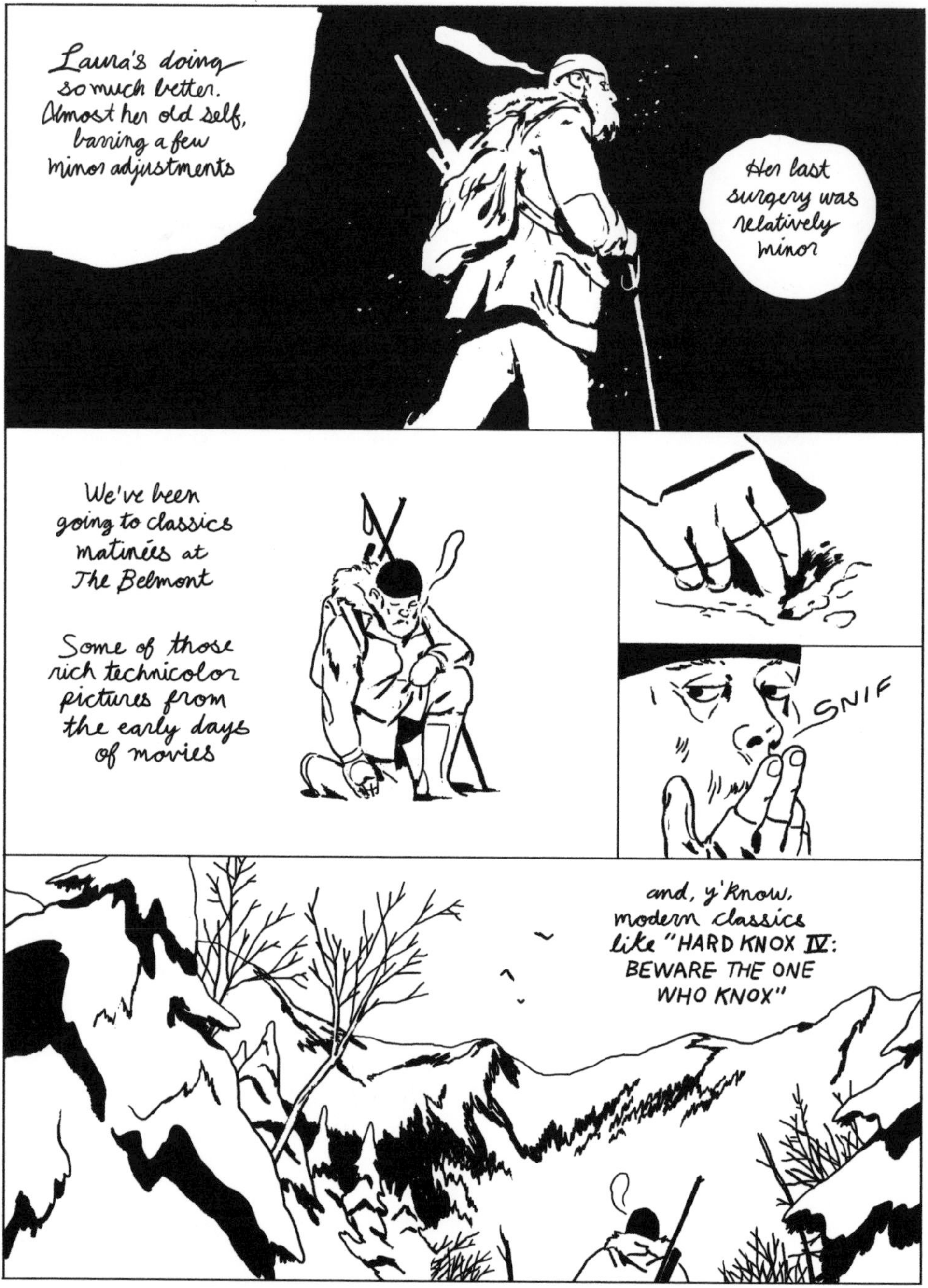
Laura's doing so much better. Almost her old self, barring a few minor adjustments
Her last surgery was relatively minor
We've been going to classics matinées at The Belmont
Some of those rich technicolor pictures from the early days of movies
SNIF
and, y'know, modern classics like "HARD KNOX IV: BEWARE THE ONE WHO KNOX"

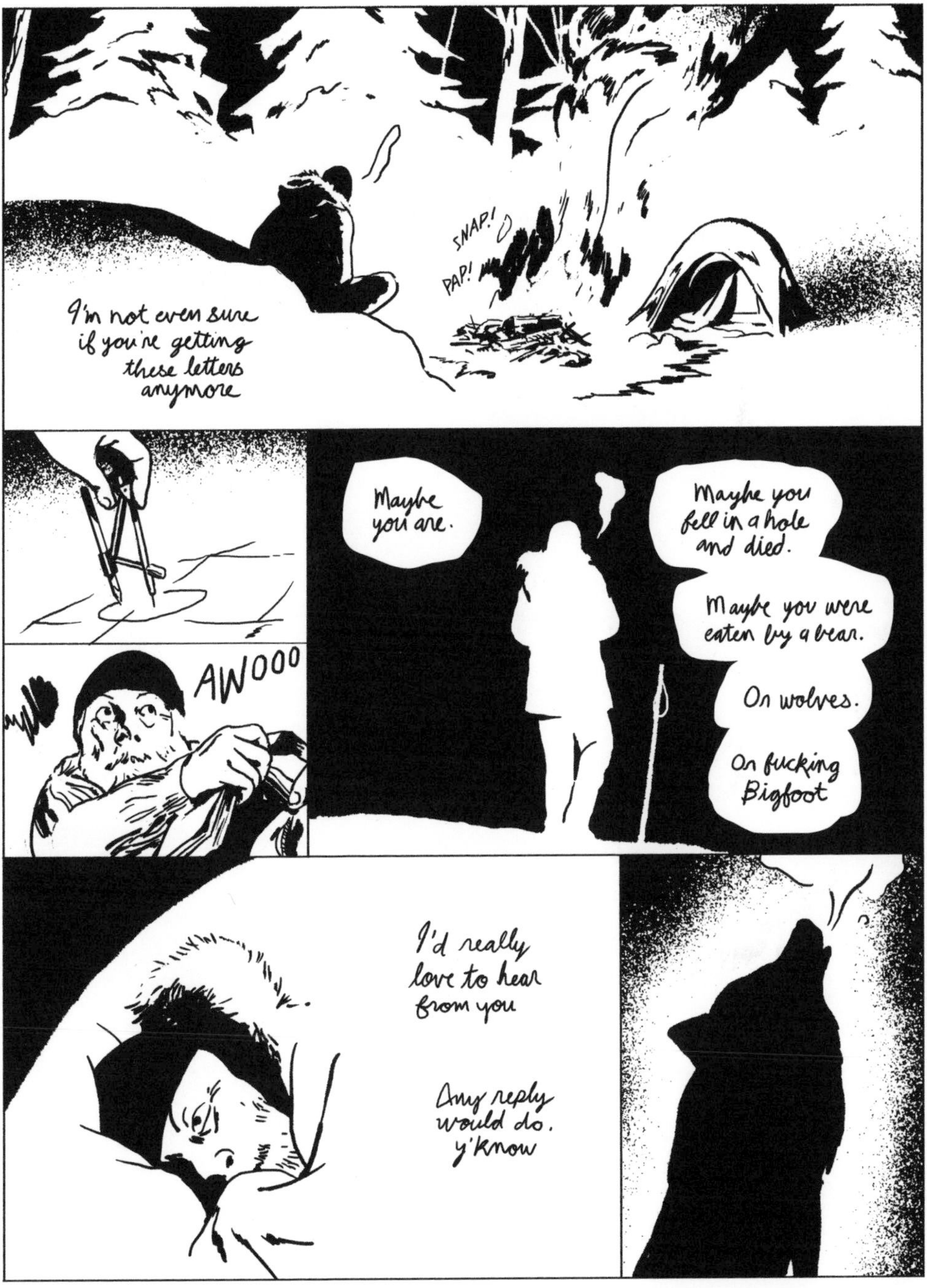
SNAP!
PAP!
I'm not even sure if you're getting these letters anymore
AWOOO
Maybe you are.
Maybe you fell in a hole and died.
Maybe you were eaten by a bear.
Or wolves.
Or fucking Bigfoot
I'd really love to hear from you
Any reply would do. y'know

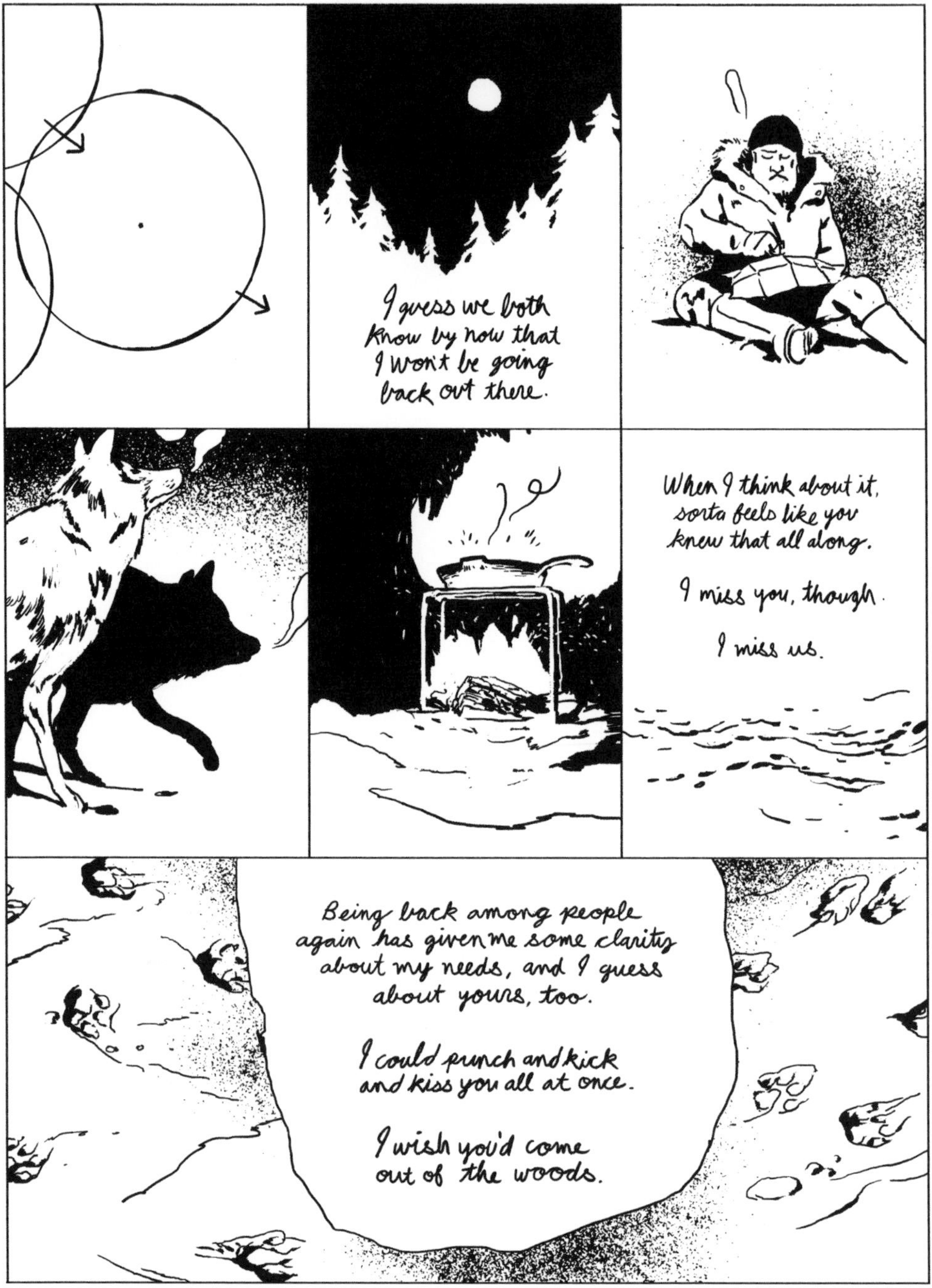
I guess we both know by now that I won't be going back out there.
When I think about it, sorta feels like you knew that all along.
I miss you, though.
I miss us.
Being back among people again has given me some clarity about my needs, and I guess about yours, too.
I could punch and kick and kiss you all at once.
I wish you'd come out of the woods.

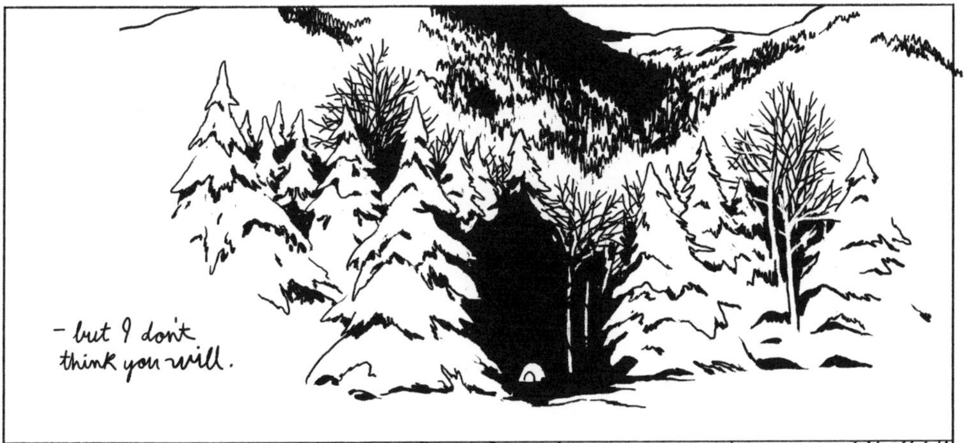
– but I don't
think you will.

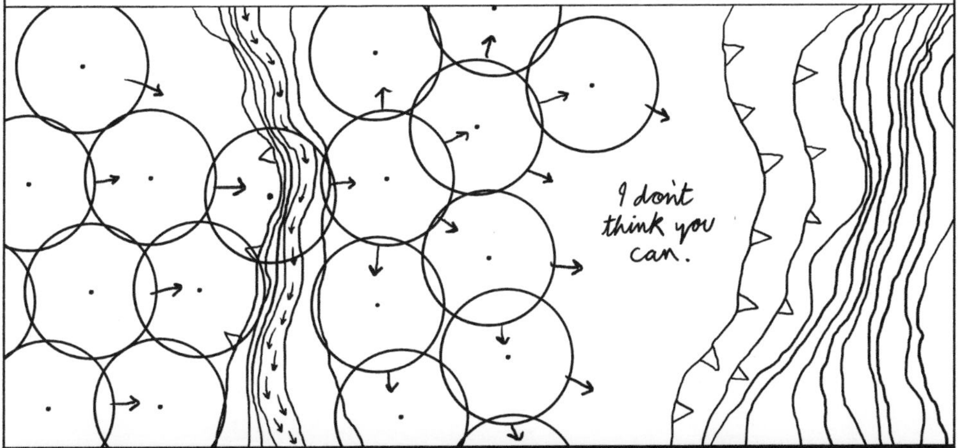
I don't
think you
can.

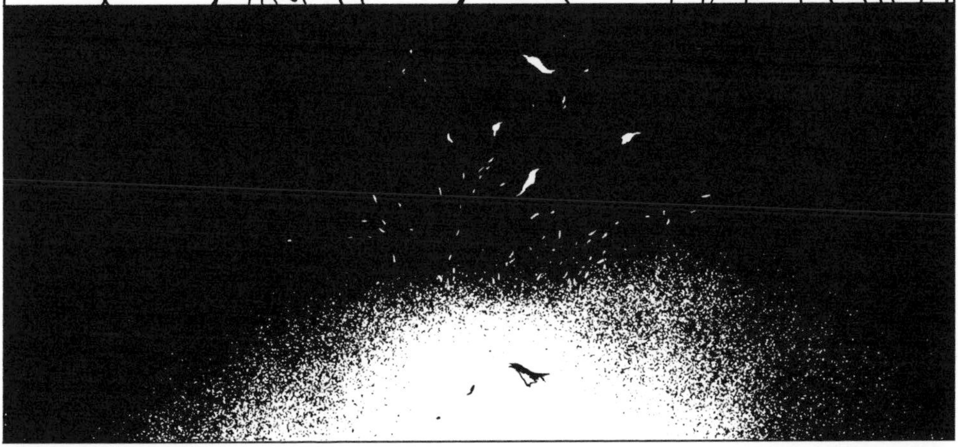

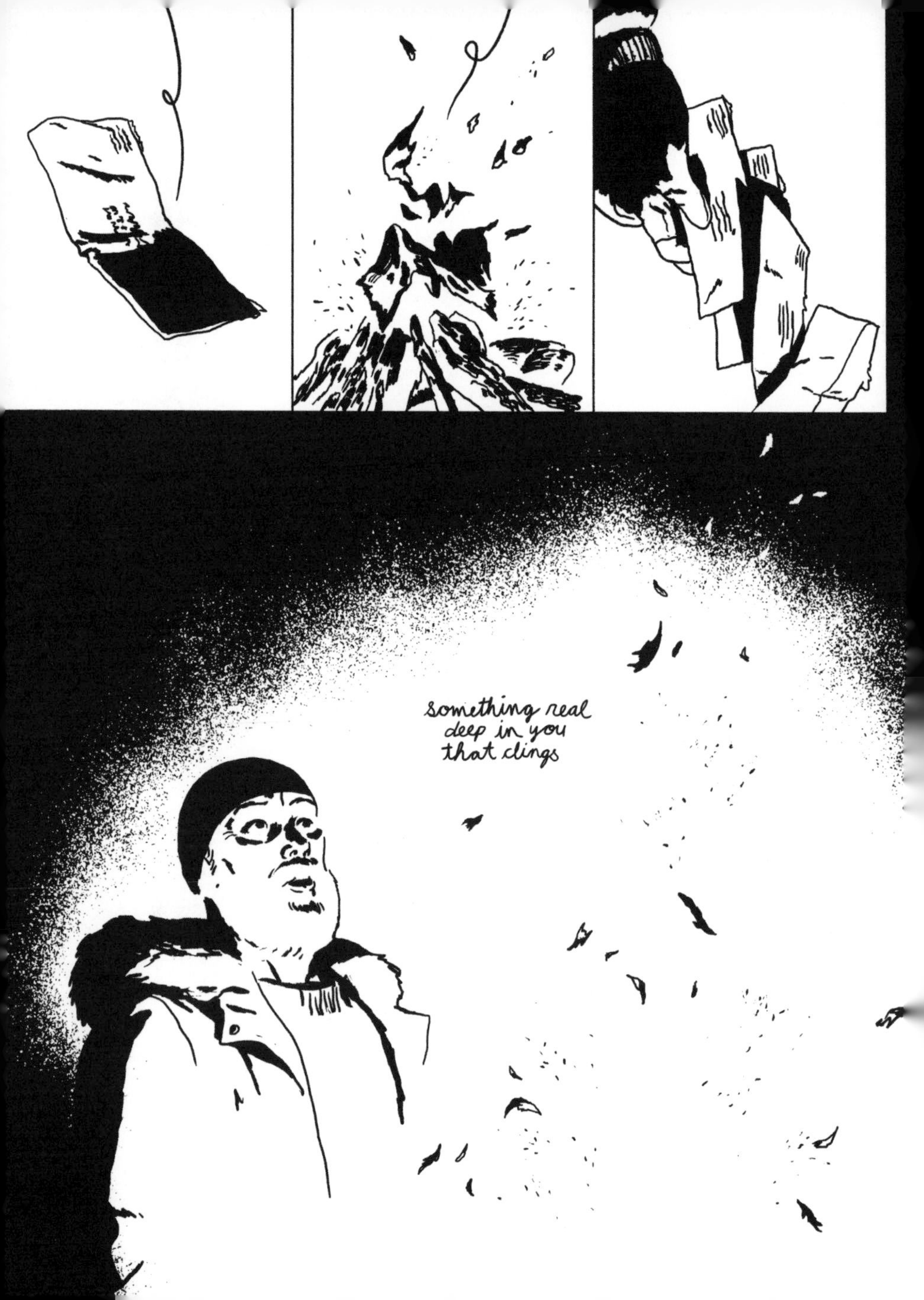
something real
deep in you
that clings

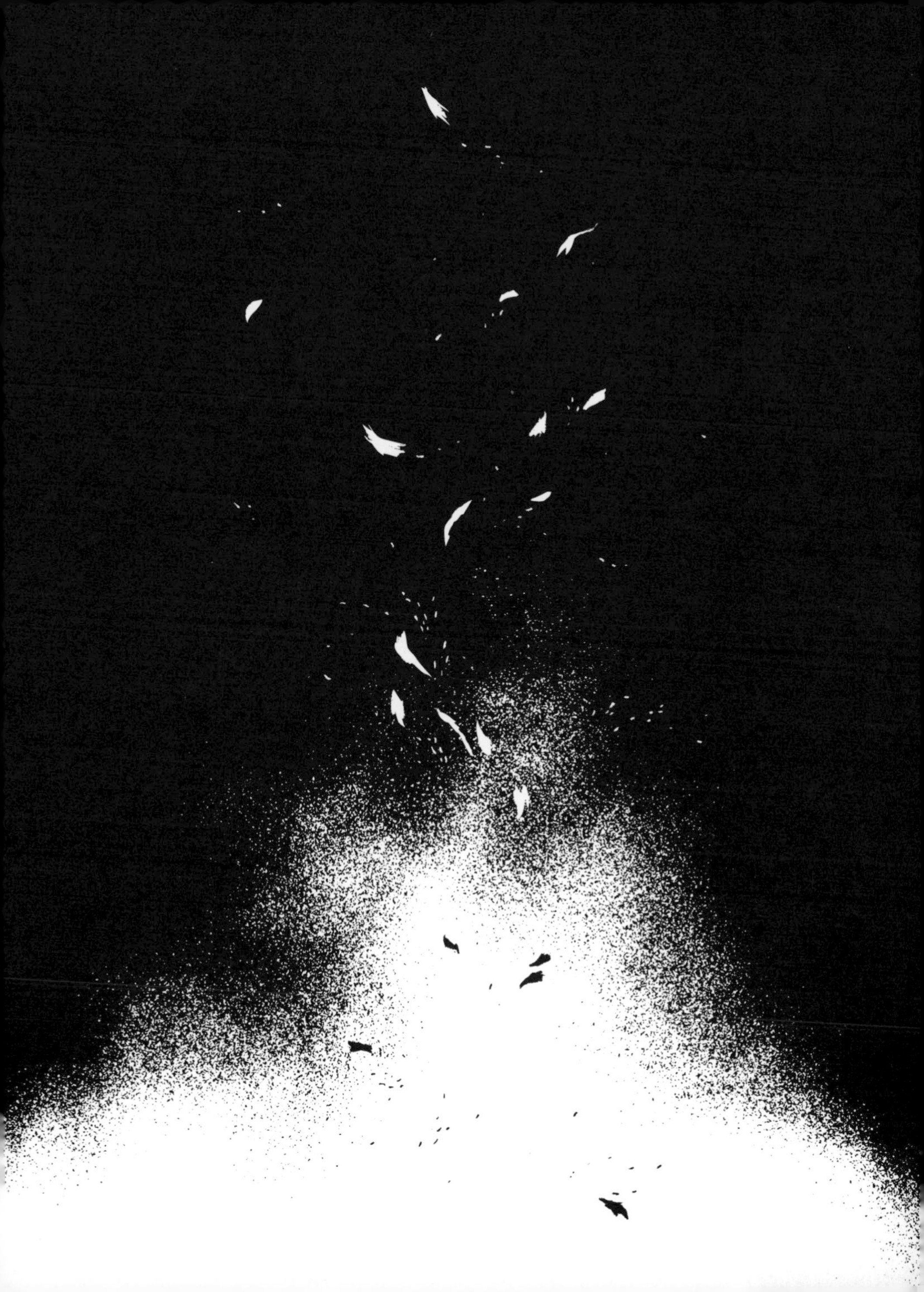

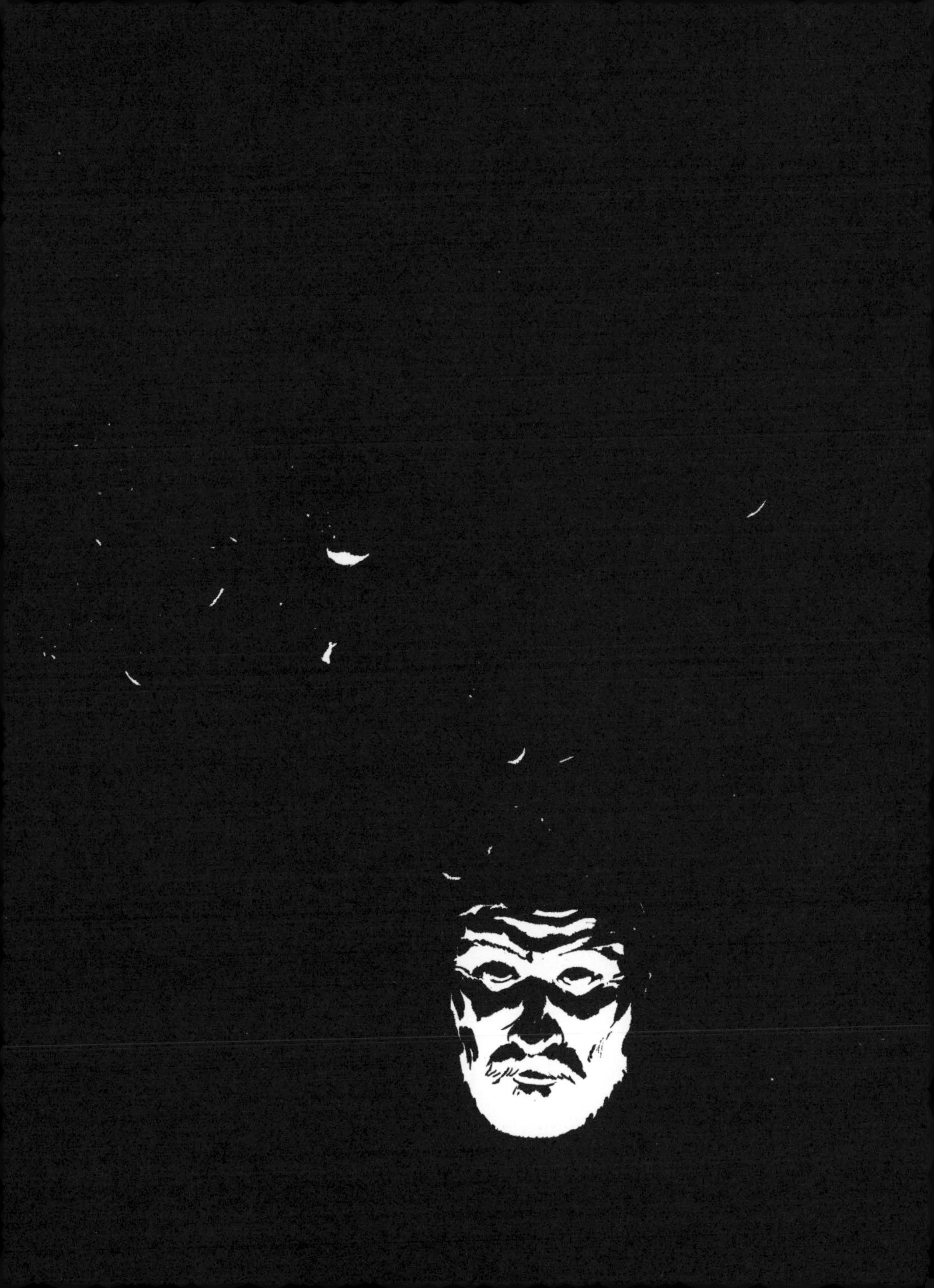

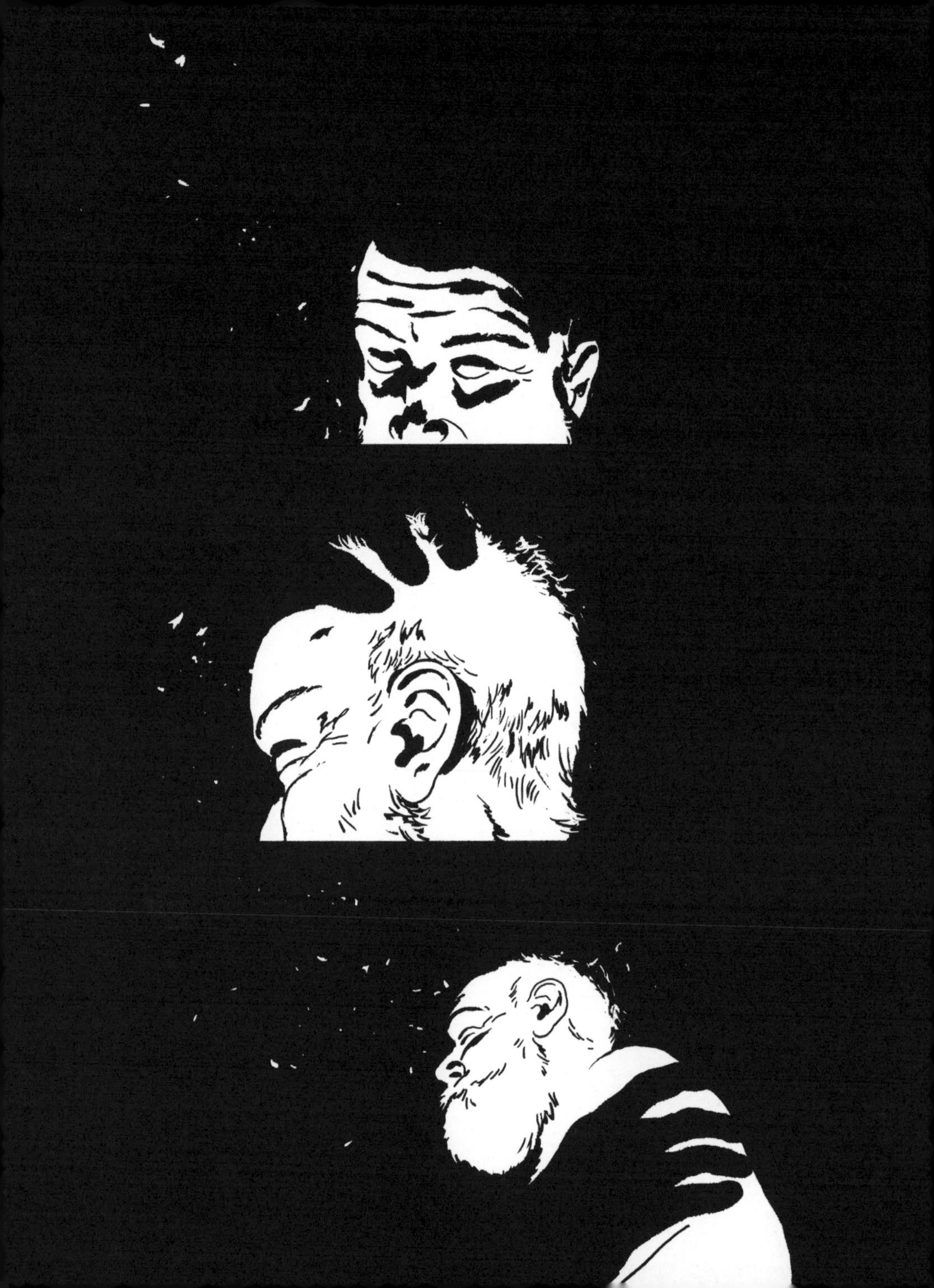

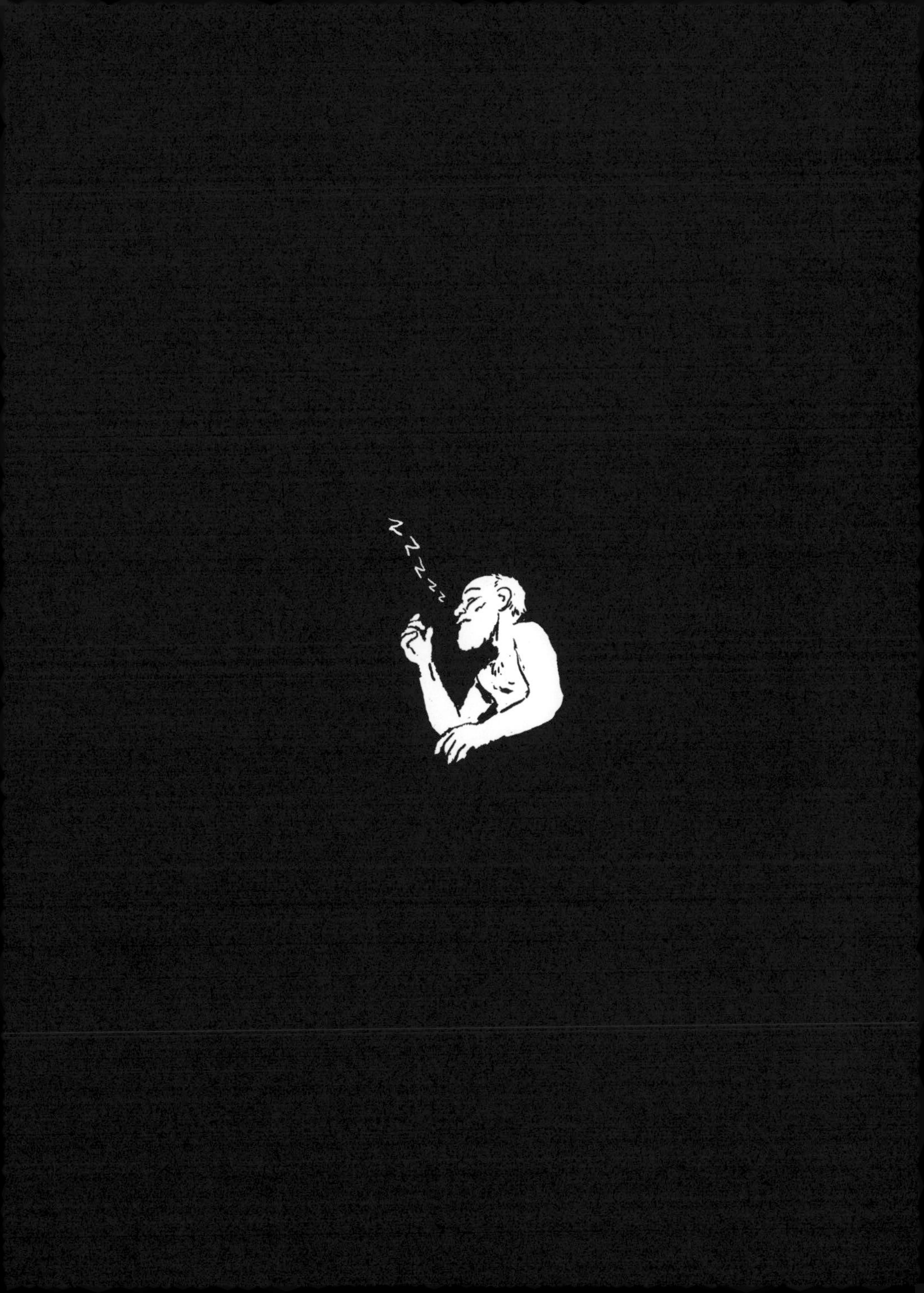
ZZZzz

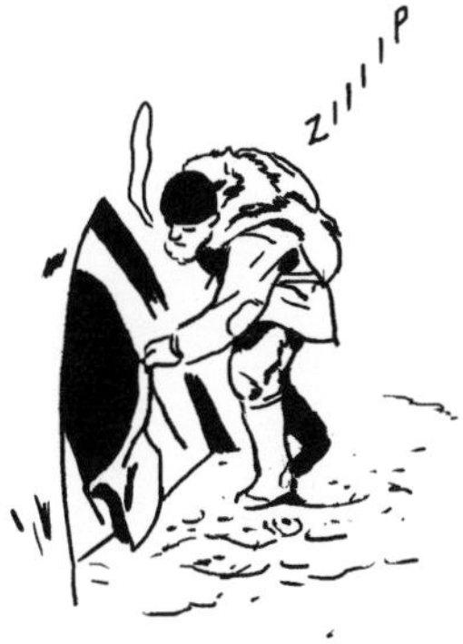
ZIIIIP

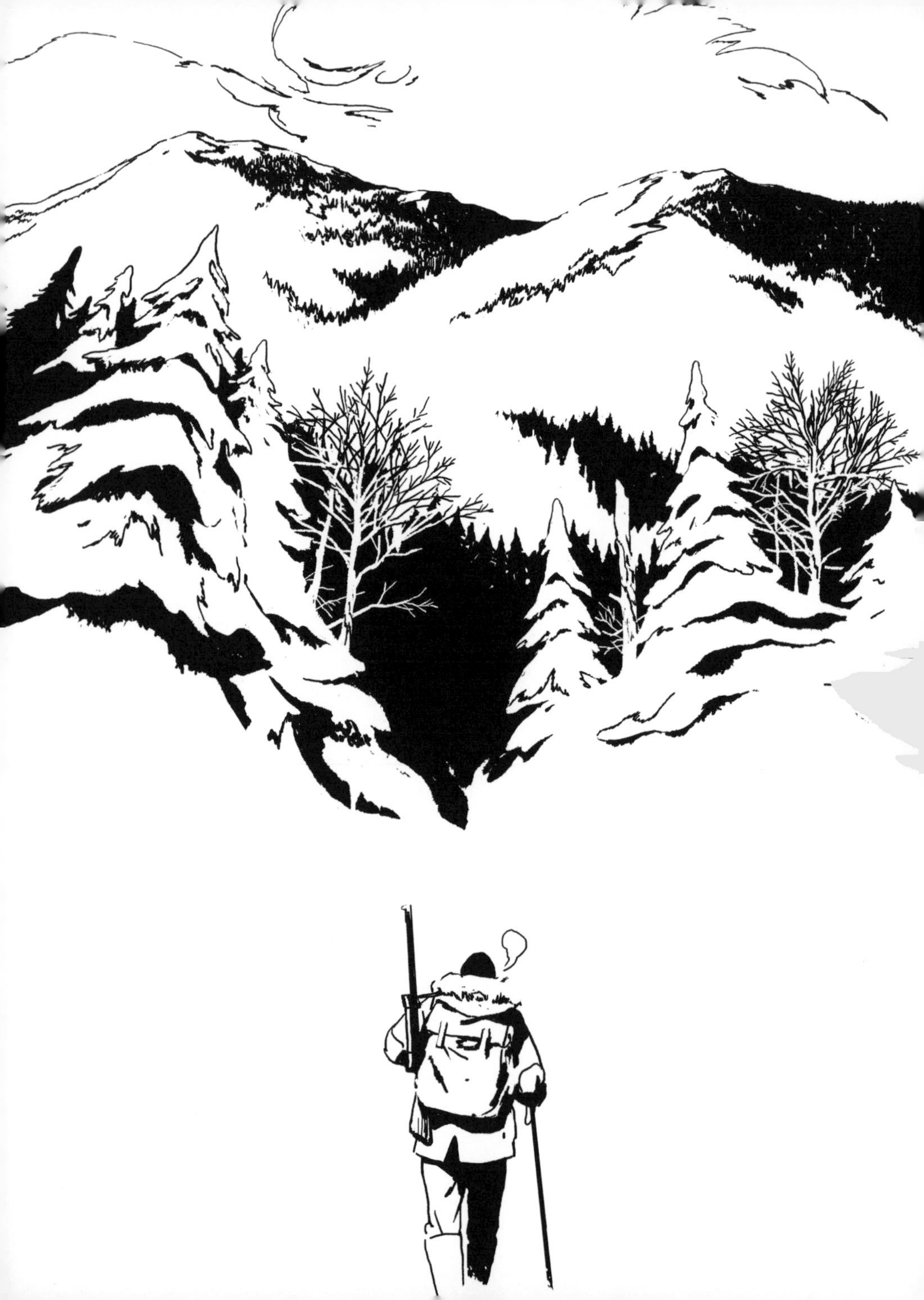

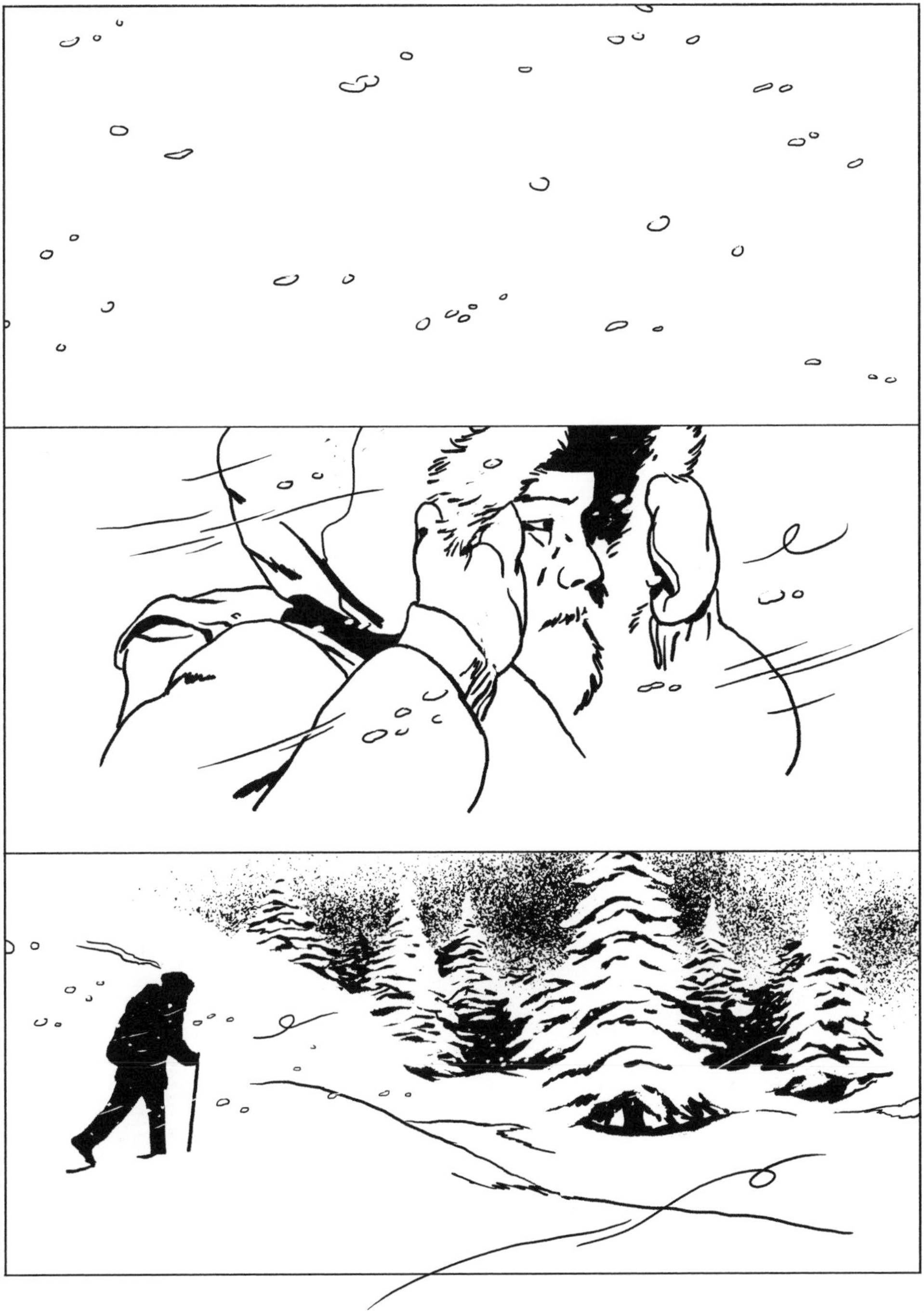

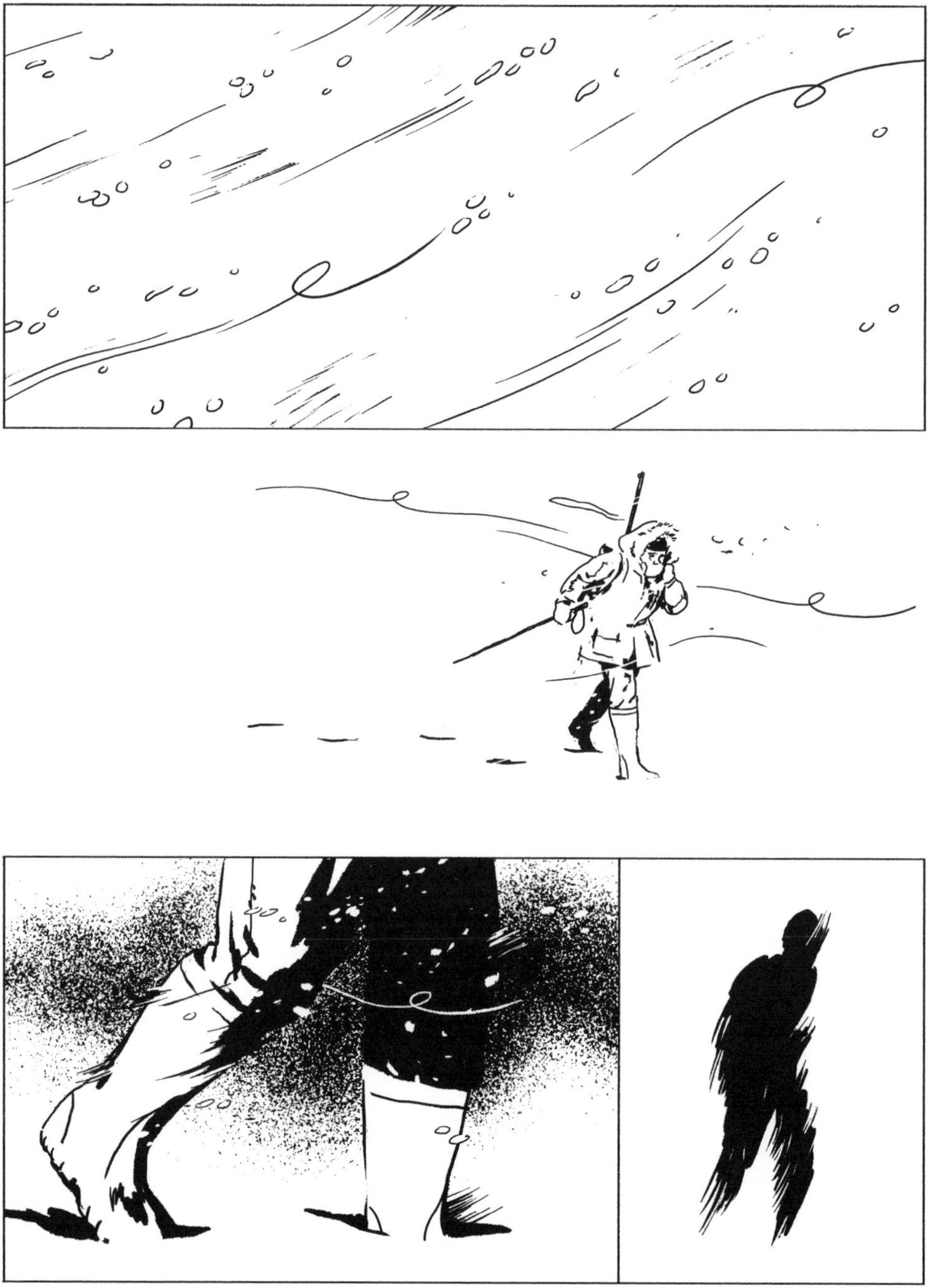

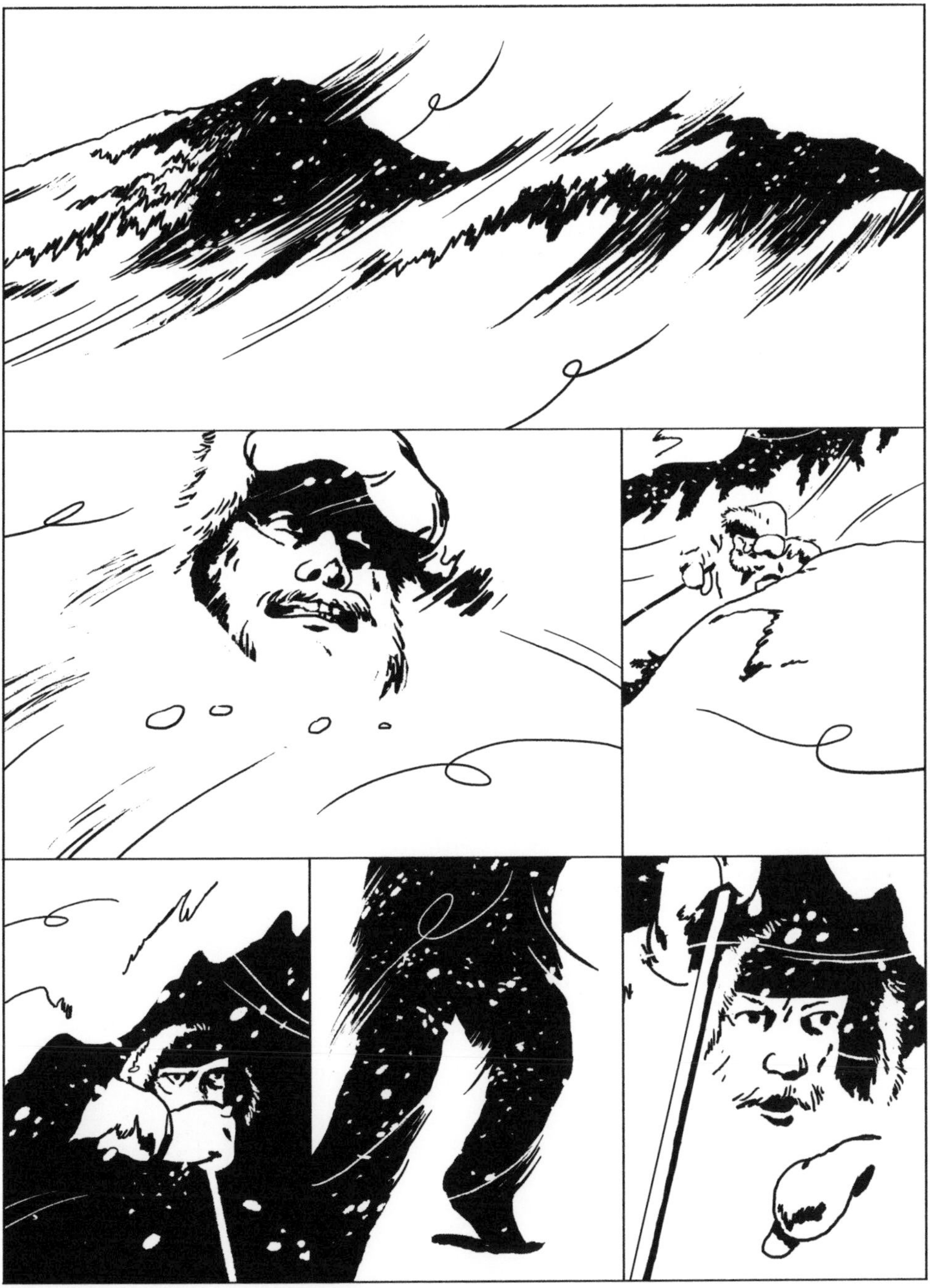

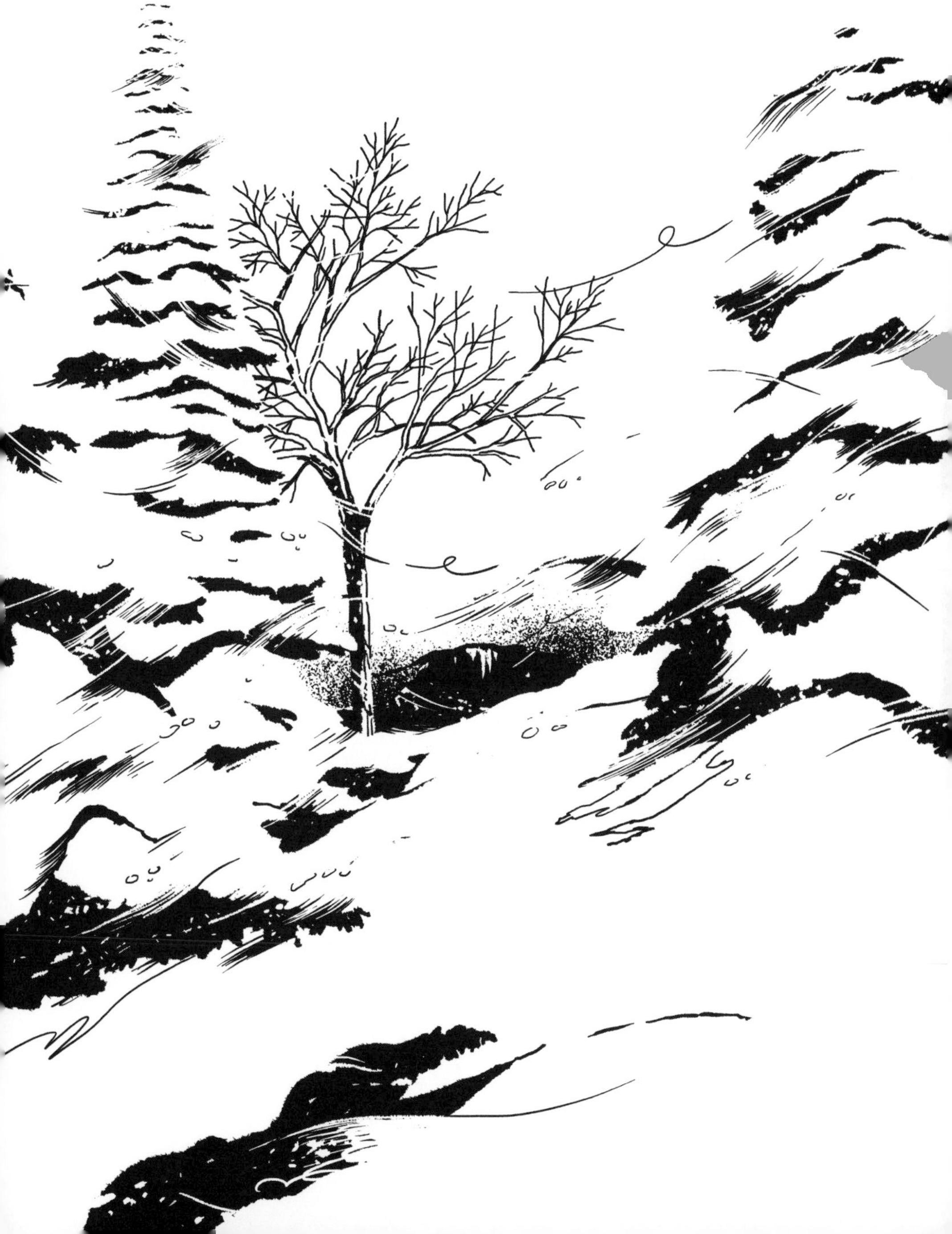

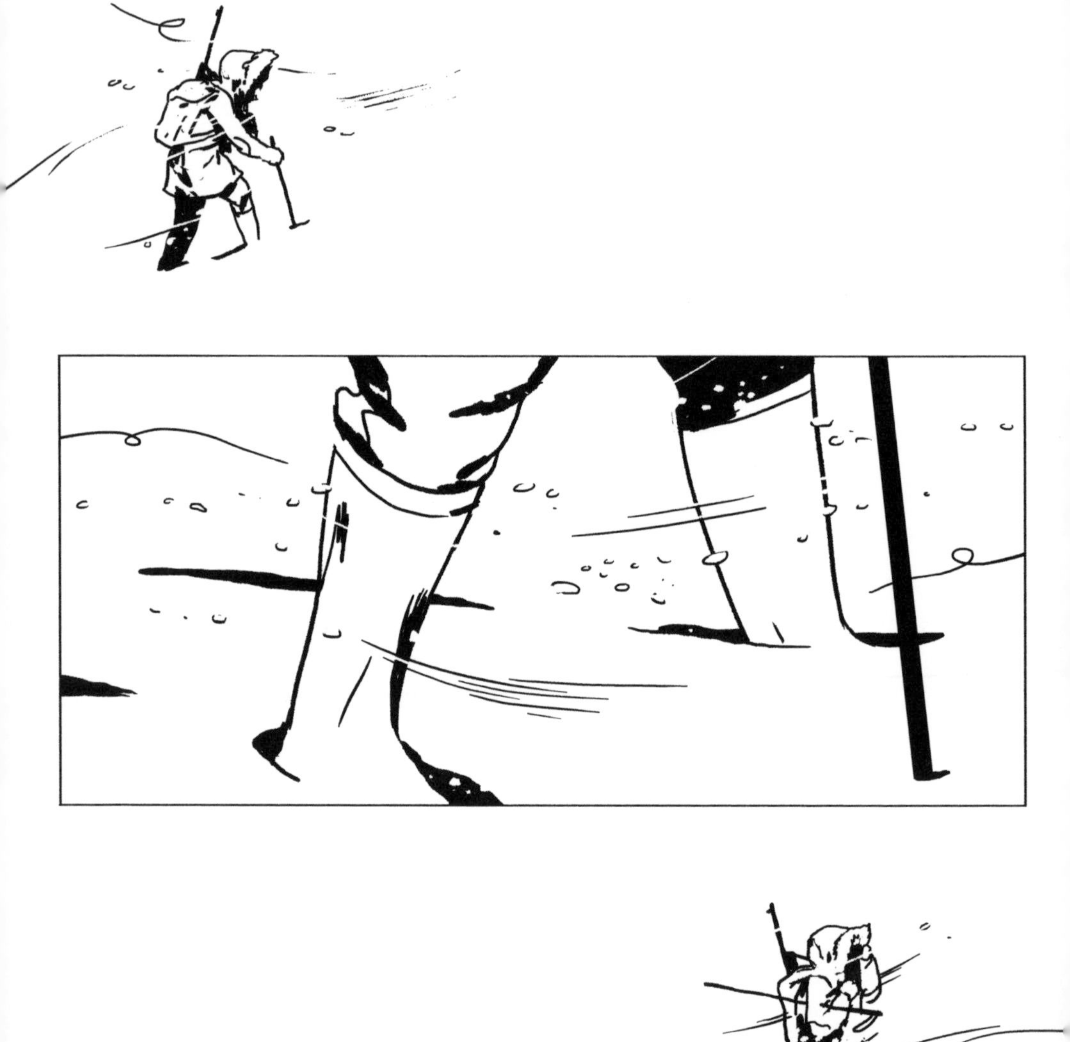

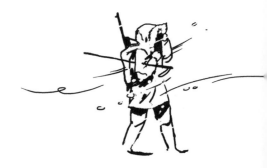

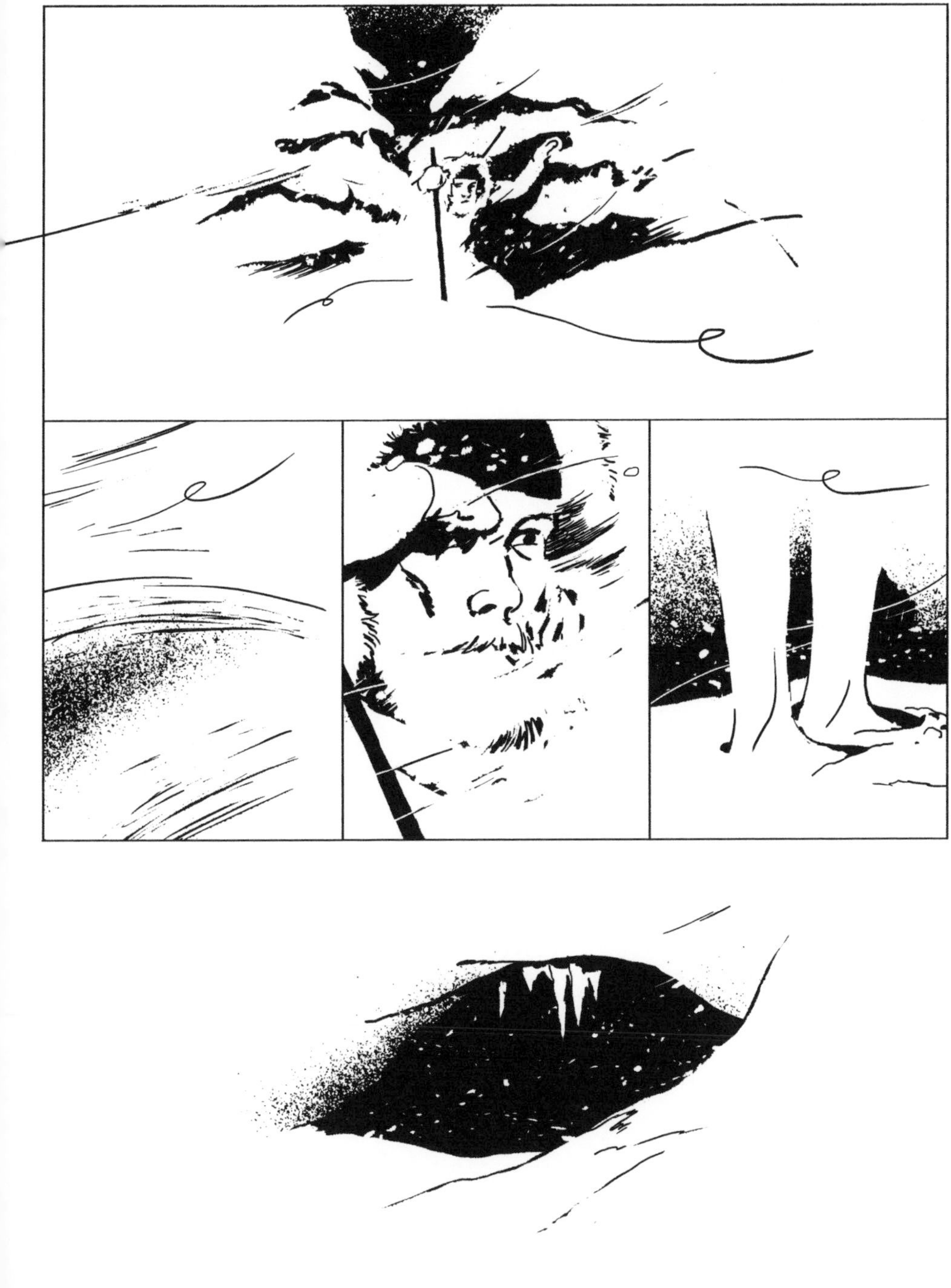

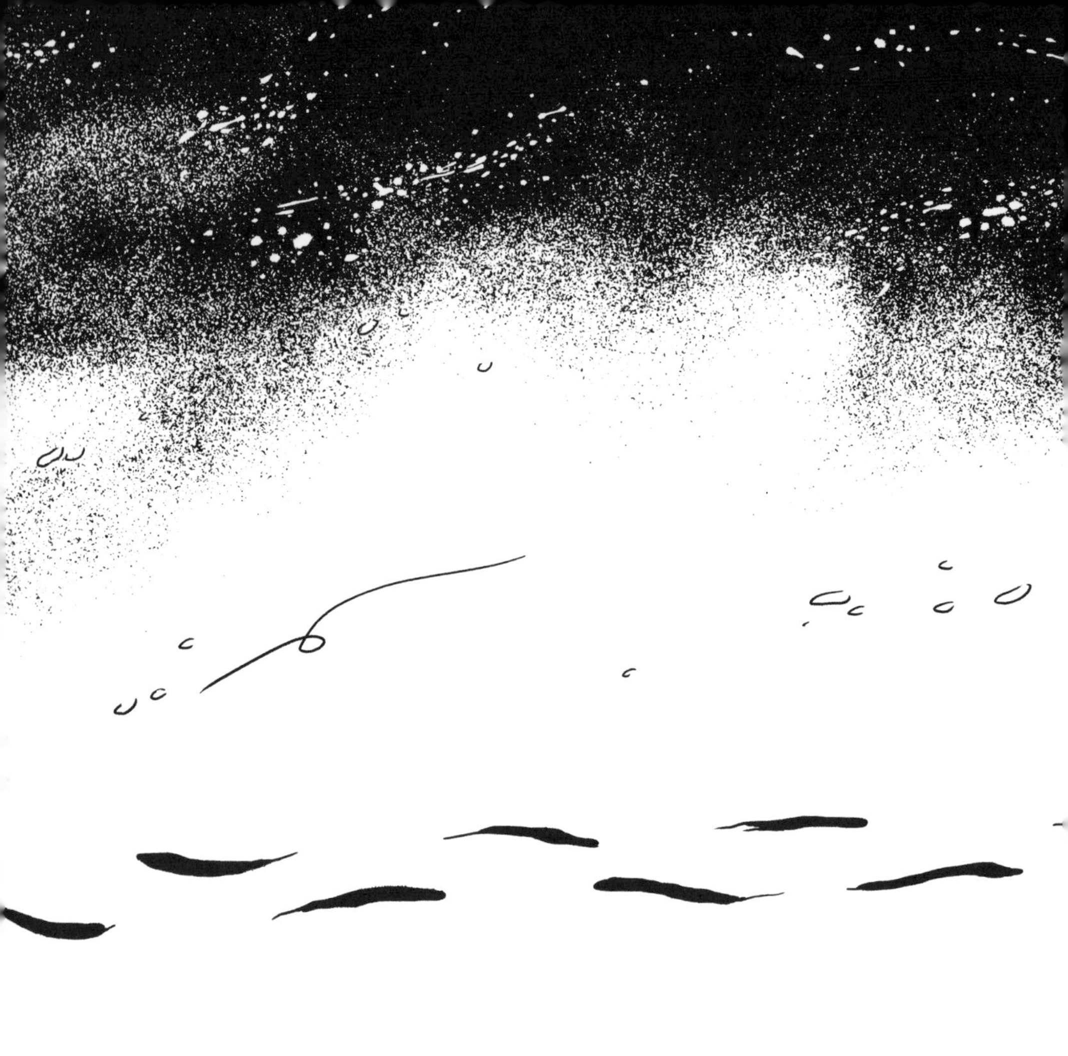

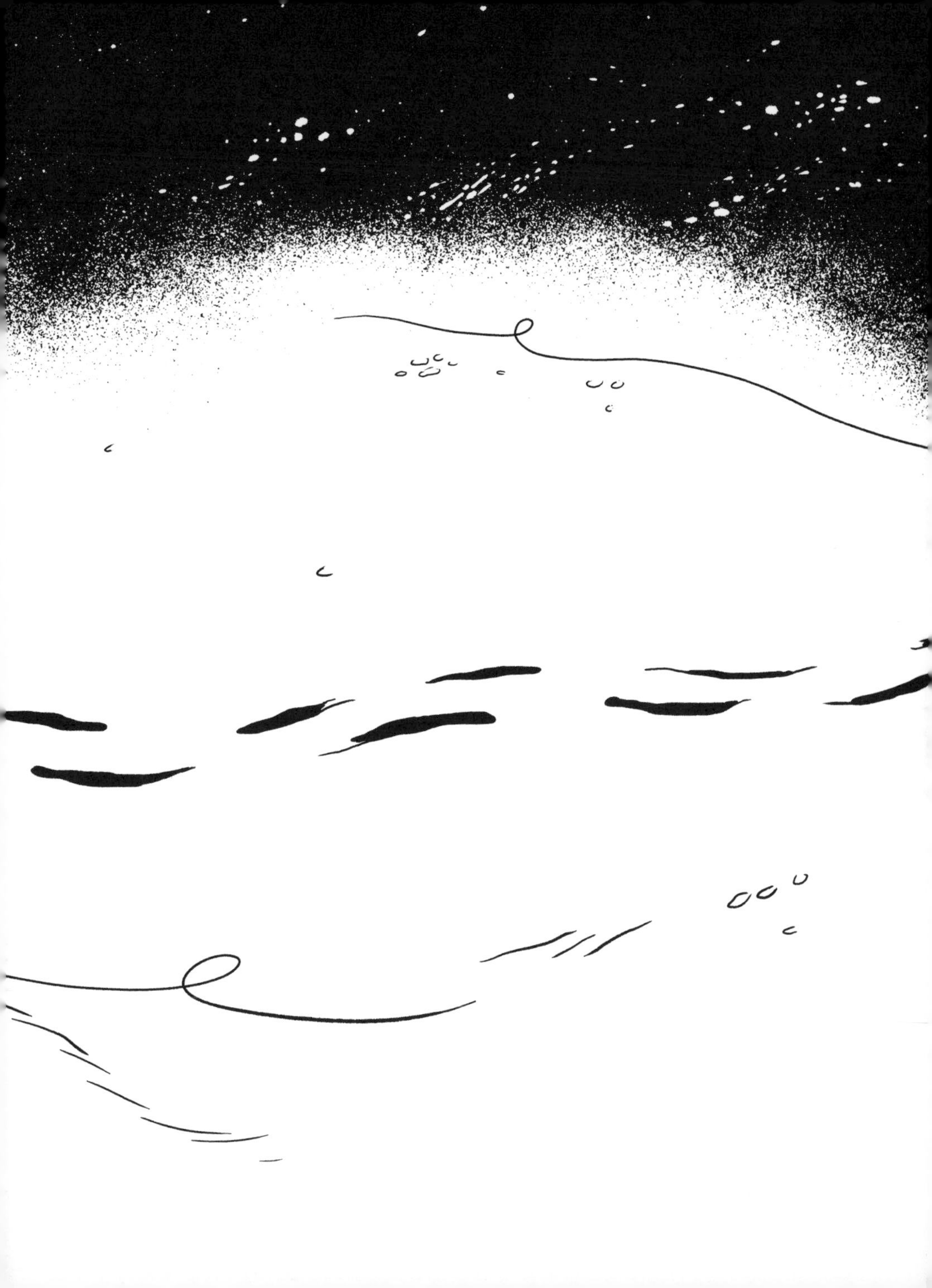

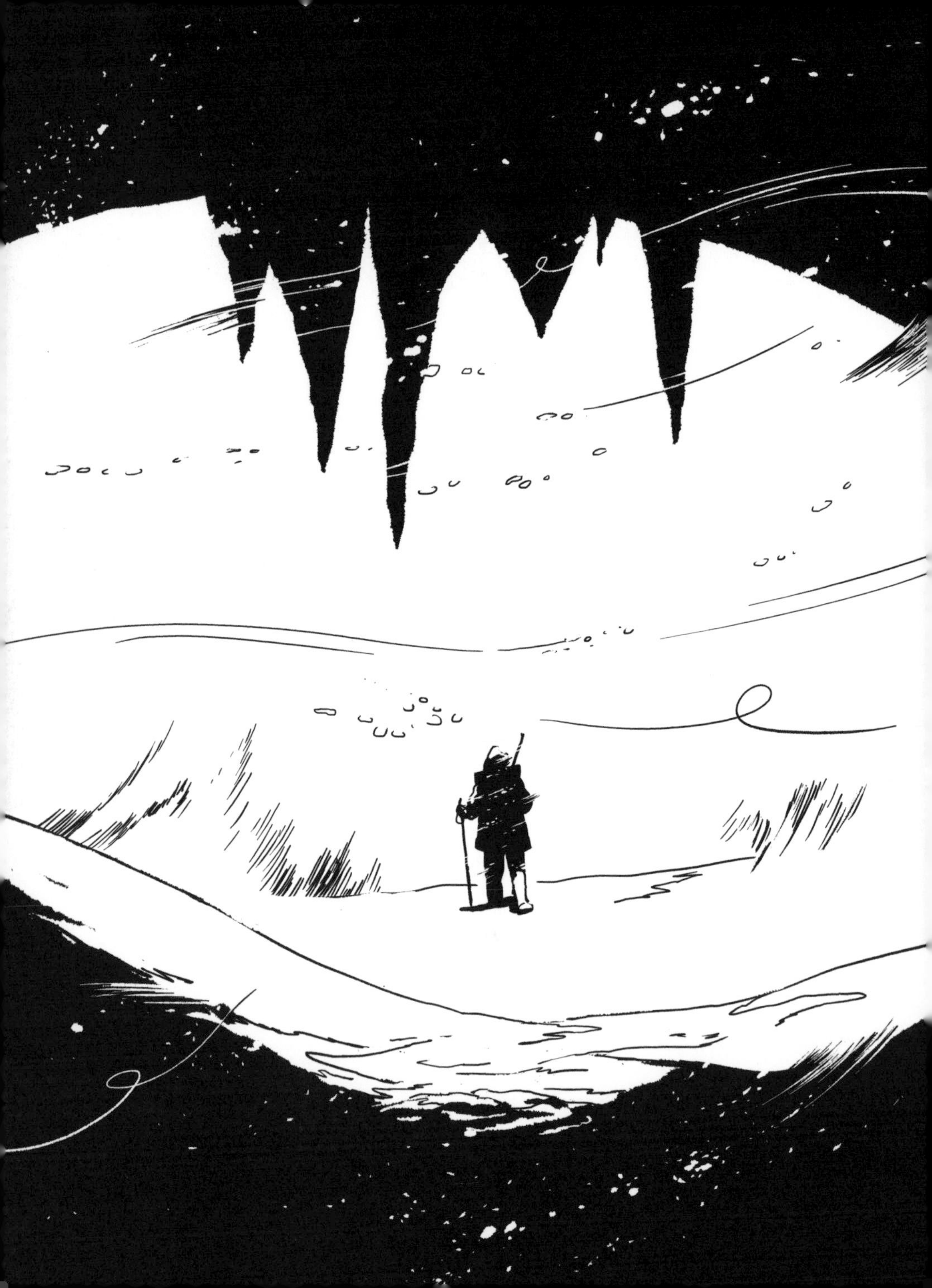

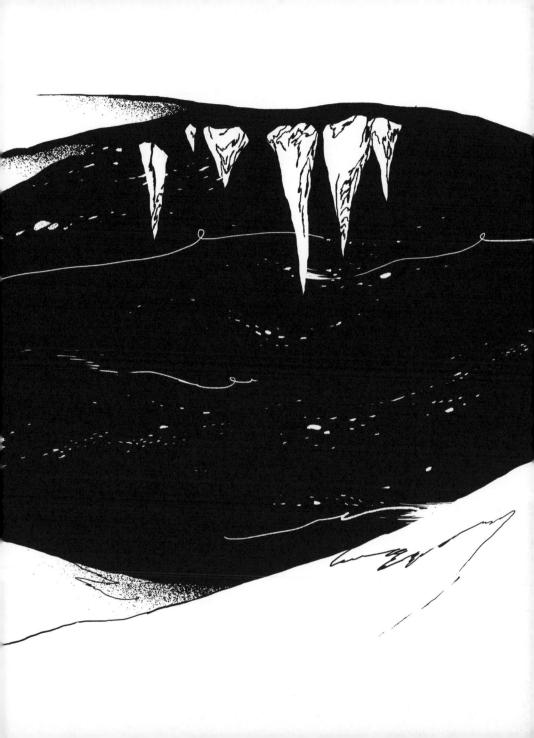

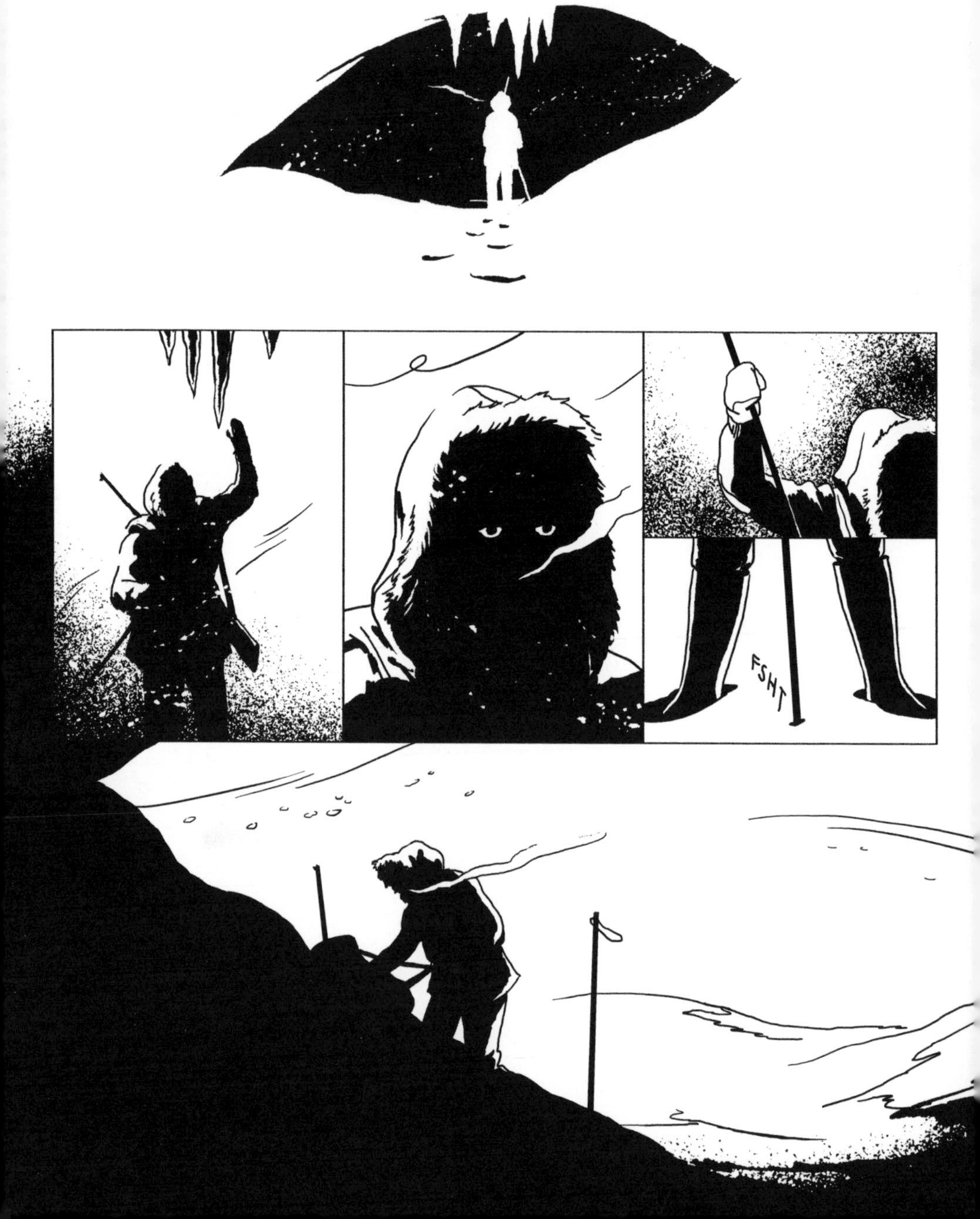
FSHT

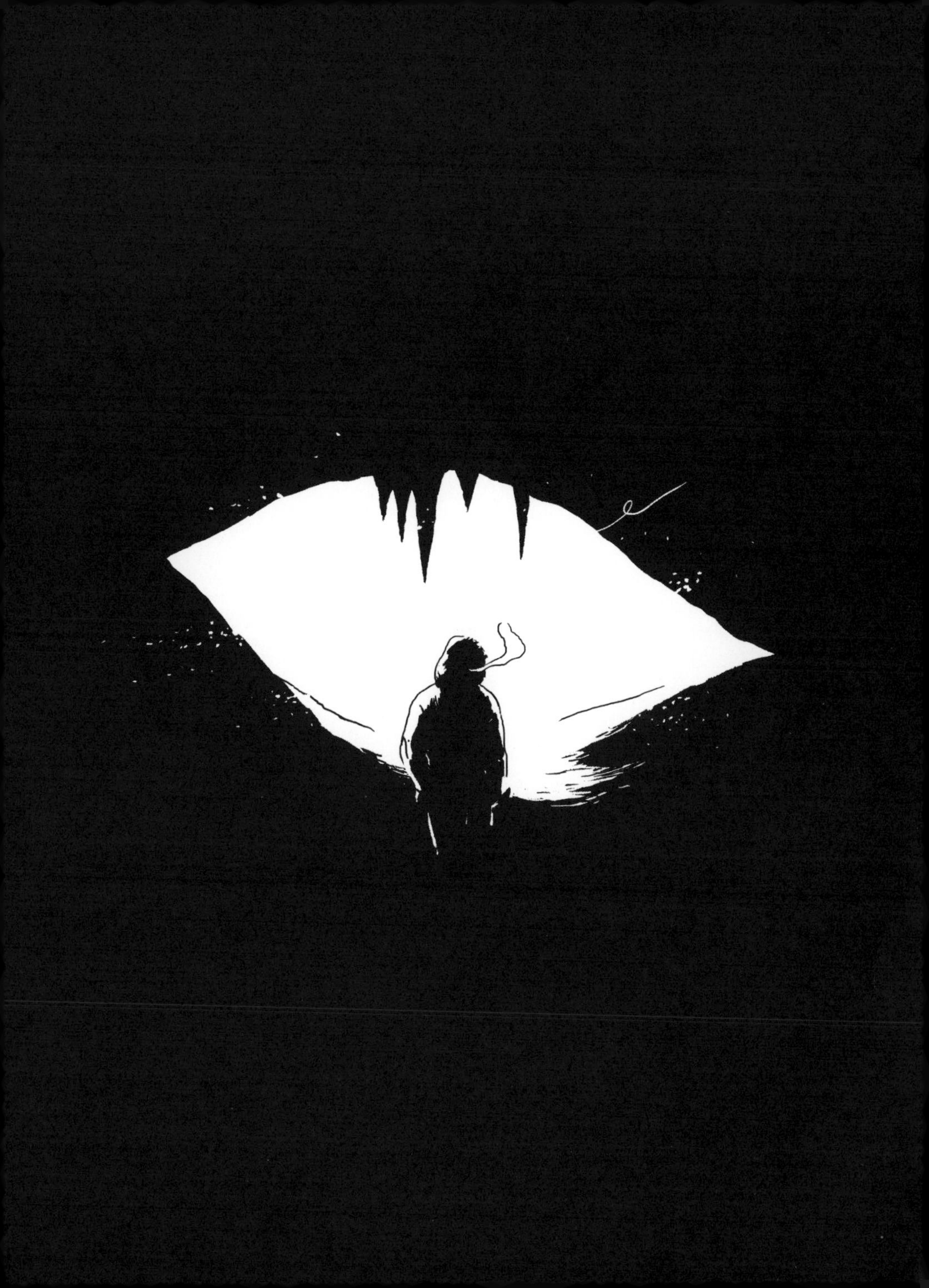

Tyler Landry lives and draws in Charlottetown, Prince Edward Island, on the east coast of Canada. Over the last 20 years, he has occupied professional roles such as Game Artist, Art Director, Illustrator, Graphic Designer, as well as Cartoonist, Club Organizer, and Comics/Drawing Instructor. These days, inching ever closer to the embrace of death, he tries to devote as much energy as possible to cartooning.

Previously published comics include: *Dungeonoids, Opal* (*Dagger Dagger* anthology), *Trabajar para Sobrevivir* (AIA Editorial), *Shit and Piss* (Retrofit Comics).